HISTORIC
SOUTH CAROLINA

HISTORIC SOUTH CAROLINA

*A Tour of the State's
Top National Landmarks*

Lee Davis Perry

Globe
Pequot

Guilford, Connecticut

Globe Pequot

An imprint of Globe Pequot, the trade division of
The Rowman & Littlefield Publishing Group, Inc.
4501 Forbes Blvd., Ste. 200
Lanham, MD 20706
www.rowman.com

Distributed by NATIONAL BOOK NETWORK

British Library Cataloguing in Publication Information available

Library of Congress Cataloging-in-Publication Data
Names: Perry, Lee Davis, author.
Title: Historic South Carolina : a tour of the state's top national
  landmarks / Lee Davis Perry.
Description: Guilford, Connecticut : Globe Pequot, [2021] | Includes index.
  | Summary: "A guide to South Carolina's historic sites"— Provided by
  publisher.
Identifiers: LCCN 2021033007 (print) | LCCN 2021033008 (ebook) | ISBN
  9781493054749 (paper ; alk. paper) | ISBN 9781493054756 (epub)
Subjects: LCSH: Historic sites—South Carolina—Guidebooks. | Historic
  buildings—South Carolina—Guidebooks. | Historic gardens—South
  Carolina —Guidebooks. | LCGFT: Guidebooks.
Classification: LCC F270 .P47 2021 (print) | LCC F270 (ebook) | DDC
  917.5704—dc23
LC record available at https://lccn.loc.gov/2021033007
LC ebook record available at https://lccn.loc.gov/2021033008

CONTENTS

CHAPTER 2: THE SOUTHERN CORNER

CHAPTER 3: THE GRAND STRAND

CHAPTER 4: THE FALL LINE

CHAPTER 5: THE UPSTATE

INTRODUCTION

First let us give some context to this geographically small state. South Carolina covers an area of about 31,000 square miles and is home to about five million people. There are forty-six separate counties, and each one believes it is significantly different from the others. This is a place where individualism flourishes and often eccentricities rule. We have been here a long time. For instance, on May 23, 1788, South Carolina was the eighth state to ratify the Constitution, which is to say that we had strong opinions at the time, and we didn't shy away from expressing them, a proclivity that is still true today. So even if our geography is small, our pride of place is large enough to more than make up for it.

If a landmark is originally defined as a mark in the landscape for guidance such as the Native Americans carving marks in trees or rocks pointing the way for their path, it also became an all-important marker for the European settlers beginning their new lives in the frontier of New World. The broader meaning now is the one covered here by the National Park Service of places in our country that have national significance for their cultural and historic value. After undergoing a rigorous nomination and recognition process, the park service selects those they consider most worthy. There are almost 2,600 of these designated sites across the nation that illustrate our heritage giving us guidance into our past...and informing our future. South Carolina has more than 70 of these sites and 65 of these have been included here. Regrettably, several are omitted because they are inaccessible due to the fragile nature of the site, perhaps suffering damage from weather or man-made catastrophes or lack of funds to stabilize them over time.

For organizational purposes the National Historic Landmarks in South Carolina are divided into five regions largely separated by historical centers of influence, terrain, and geography. There's Charleston and the Surrounding Area where the lion's share of landmarks are located; it got the earliest start (1670) on settlement in the English colony and held onto dominance as a center of trade and political thought. Next is the Southern Corner, part of the Carolina Lowcountry along the lower section of the coast; it is centered around Beaufort (1711), a smaller but significant port of commerce in the state's development. The upper coastline is the area called The Grand Strand (today's sandy stretch of beach) where Georgetown (1729) flourished with its concentration of surrounding rice fields generating vast wealth for early South Carolinians. Moving inland is The Fall Line or the Midlands, named for

Spanish moss draping live oak trees is an iconic image in South Carolina.

its geographical separation between the Lowcountry where the land is low, flat, and sandy and The Upstate, which is higher, rocky, and hilly. The Fall Line's geographic and political center is Columbia (1786), the state capital. And The Upstate or Piedmont where settlers sought to carve out a living among the foothills of the Blue Ridge Mountains, and which later gave rise to the economic success of the textile industry, is centered around Greenville (1797) and Spartanburg (1831).

There is a Thematic Index included in the back of the book that provides a quick overview of all the sites by various categories. By far Architecturally Significant is the largest group due to the concentration of wealth in South Carolina leading up to the Civil War. This prosperity was expressed through fine 18th- and 19th-century architecture in Charleston and beyond. Less visible is that the majority of this wealth was generated through its agricultural successes of rice, indigo, and cotton made possible by large numbers of enslaved African Americans as the labor force. Both free and enslaved people were the skilled craftspeople that physically built the mansions and important public buildings, too. Now these contributions are gradually coming to light as more research is digging deeper to uncover their lost stories. The African American and Civil Rights History category lists those sites that are attempting to tell the whole story and will hopefully include many more of these significant sites among South Carolina's National Historic Landmarks in the future. The Native American and Early Peoples' list is short, but as more of their history is traced their cultural impact on our state will be recognized. Sadly, there weren't currently enough Women's sites to warrant a separate group, but again this may change in the future. The other groupings hope to appeal to your specific interests so that you may design your own travels through time.

A couple more words of guidance as you begin to investigate these pages. Know that the "facts" presented here are based on diverse reliable source material that often gave diverse information. It seems that versions of the "truth" are inevitable when you are reaching back into 300 (or even several thousands of) years of history. Every effort was made to confirm names, dates, and events, but many choices had to be made based on purely personal selections. Hopefully, the overall version presented may inspire further study by you so that you may form your own version of the "truth" gaining greater insight and perspective into our states and nation's colorful history.

And lastly, as we go to press, the Covid-19 pandemic is still widespread altering our world in unprecedented ways. Tourism has been affected greatly. Many of the sites have closed temporarily or have limited hours; some have kept surrounding grounds open if not indoor sites, but all need support to recover from revenue losses. Be sure to consult their websites or other contact information to determine their status. Days and hours listed are from pre-pandemic times, so double-check before planning to visit. But, do visit!

Also, many of the homes and other sites are privately owned, so feel free to view them from the sidewalk or street respecting the privacy of the owner and their careful stewardship of the property. However, do immerse yourself in these pages and take an armchair or actual tour of Historic South Carolina's Top National Landmarks while learning about some of the people, places, and events that shaped our great country. I hope you find it to be an engaging and rewarding experience; I know I certainly did.

William Aiken House and
Associated Railroad Structures
Tina E. Mayland

Chapter 1
CHARLESTON & THE SURROUNDING AREA

William Aiken House and Associated Railroad Structures
456 King St., Charleston; 843-853-1810; pphgcharleston.com; limited access

The William Aiken House is an impressive home located a few blocks north of Calhoun Street and the city's downtown historic area at the corner of King and Ann Streets. Built in 1807 it is a wood frame Charleston single house in the Federal Adamesque style. The three-story building has a two-story piazza (porch) facing the lovely garden. An octagonal ballroom addition and a Gothic Revival carriage house were added sometime after 1831. It was severely damaged in the Charleston 1886 earthquake, but much of its intricate woodwork and elegant architectural features remain. The house is named for William Aiken Sr., father of South Carolina governor, William Aiken Jr. Aiken Sr. was born in County Antrim, Ireland, immigrated to America, and purchased the home in 1811 for $14,000.

Aiken was the first president of the South Carolina Canal and Railroad Company started in 1827. The port of Savannah held a competitive edge in the shipping trade, and the new company sought to regain some of this business, an ongoing competition between the ports of Savannah and Charleston that continues to this day. The rail lines were constructed during 1830–1833, completing the track to Hamburg, SC (now Aiken), some 136 miles away, and connecting the port to inland markets. This marked the longest length of track under single management in the world at the time.

Unfortunately, Aiken Sr. was unable to enjoy the results of this feat due to his accidental death; one day in 1831 construction noise frightened the horses pulling his carriage and it overturned. Another setback was the explosion of the first American-made steam locomotive. The South Carolina Canal and Railroad Company had commissioned the locomotive with a New York manufacturer who shipped the pieces to Charleston for reassembly. The locomotive made history on Christmas Day 1830, when it traveled at an astonishing speed of 12–15 mph and a distance of six whole miles (the length of track laid to date) and became America's first regularly scheduled railroad with its subsequent runs. Six months into its rail service, an operator error caused the boiler to explode at one of its stops, only temporarily marring the success of this new form of transportation for commercial and passenger traffic. (A full-scale replica is on view at the South Carolina State Museum in Columbia.) Later, the railroad company became part of the Norfolk Southern Company operation.

The associated railroad structures are the Camden Depot (1850), Deans Warehouse (1856), South Carolina Railroad Warehouse (1857), Tower Passenger Depot (1850), Line Streetcar and Carpenter Shops (1857), and the railroad right-of-way. All together, these buildings make up the best example of an antebellum railroad terminal facility.

The William Aiken House and surrounding property is currently operated as an event venue by Patrick Properties Hospitality Group, who has meticulously restored and furnished it as a period-appropriate house.

William Blacklock House
18 Bull St., Charleston; 843-953-5773; cofc.edu; limited access

Successful British merchant, William Blacklock, built his stately home in 1800 in the Adamesque style after previously purchasing two lots in the newly laid out "suburb" of Harleston Village, just outside the Charleston mercantile district. Blacklock's wealth was accumulated through his partnership with Adam Tunno, a Scots merchant with whom he ran one of the major import-export businesses along the city's waterfront. They prospered along with Charleston's seaport prominence, and his home reflects the sophisticated and refined tastes of the period and is one of the largest homes in the city.

The two-story residence sits atop a high brick basement made of Charleston grey brick (brown in color) laid in the Flemish bond pattern. The house fronts the sidewalk, set back only the width of a matching double flight of stairs with wrought-iron railings leading to the front entrance. The central double doorway with delicate sidelight windows is topped by a lovely elliptical fanlight window. The flanking windows are recessed in bays with round-arched tops. Flat lintels and marble keystones are incorporated into the other windows. The house has a hipped roof with the gable end featuring a large lunette fanlight.

The interior showcases richly detailed woodwork and plasterwork with longleaf pine floors and cypress paneling in some rooms. An elegantly proportioned vaulted ceiling complements the circular staircase. A detailed 1816 inventory of Blacklock's estate describes the layout and room usage with the dining room and parlor fronting the first floor (above the ground level basement) with a bed chamber and servant's

William Blacklock House, Charleston
Tina E. Mayland

room behind them, and a drawing room, two bed chambers, and a nursery on the floor above.

The architect is unknown but many suspect that Gabriel Manigault (see Manigault House below) was involved. Manigault was selected as the designer of the US Bank building, now City Hall (at Charleston's famous Four Corners of Law). Blacklock was on the board of the Branch Bank of the United States in Charleston and served on the building committee for the project, establishing a connection between the two men. Also, architecturally, the Tuscan columns used in the house are similar to ones that appear in another Manigault structure, the Orphan House Chapel. The property's two outbuildings in the rear garden are in the Gothic Revival style.

A major restoration of the Blacklock House took place in 1937 by E. des Brosses Hunter. The house was acquired by the College of Charleston (see below) in 1974 as a part of their campus in the center of the city, and currently serves as their Office of Alumni Relations. There is limited access to the public.

Miles Brewton House
27 King St., Charleston; privately owned

Remarkably, this stunning brick residence on lower King Street has stayed in the same family since it was completed in 1769. And equally remarkable may be that one of the most architecturally significant houses in Charleston has also survived wars, fires, and hurricanes with its beauty intact. Wealthy merchant Miles Brewton most certainly would be proud. He inherited the land from his prosperous grandfather and father and, based on trips to Europe, knew the style he wanted for his showplace home. He co-designed the house with woodworker Ezra Waite in the Palladian style originally created by Andrea Palladio for villas outside Venice, Italy, some 500 years ago. The symmetrical plan and the front-facing double portico reflect the revival of the Old-World style popular in British country houses at the beginning of the 18th century. Soon thereafter, pattern books came to the colonies and influenced architectural tastes. The balance is evident in the "double house" design with four main rooms on each floor divided by a central stair hall. In addition to Waite, master carvers John Lord and Thomas Woodin from London are believed responsible for the woodwork in the upstairs drawing room. Magnificent may not be adequate to describe the Georgian interiors they created over the four years of construction.

On the exterior the two-story house is elevated by a high stone basement flanked on either side with matching marble staircases leading to the portico. The symmetrical portico is crafted with Doric columns on the first level rising to Ionic columns on the upper level supporting a richly detailed pedimented roof. The street-front iron fence is topped by a *chevaux-de-frise*, or 18th-century security device of sharp points projecting outward from a central rod, grabbing the attention of many a tourist and other passersby. Recent owners completed a heavily researched and detailed restoration of the house in 1988–92.

The provenance of the house lends interesting history to its story as well. The prominence of the house made it the desired location for occupation forces as military headquarters during both the Revolutionary and Civil wars. Tradition tells us that Rebecca Brewton Motte, who inherited the property after her brother's untimely death at sea in 1775, hosted British commanders, Sir Henry Clinton, Lord Francis Rawdon, and General Cornwallis among them. Her late husband had served as provincial treasurer, but her loyalties now sided with the patriots. She entertained the officers lavishly while essentially serving as a captive in her own home. And she secretly hid her three young daughters in the attic for many months away from any interaction with the British soldiers below. But the soldiers left their marks of graffiti

Miles Brewton House, Charleston
Tina E. Mayland

PRIVATE RESIDENCE

including a nicely rendered warship sketched into the marble fireplace surround in the downstairs parlor. Ah, the secrets these walls could reveal . . .

Beyond the rear garden original outbuildings on the north side of the property include a kitchen, laundry, and carriage house. Just behind the kitchen is an arcade of storerooms, stables, and a two-story structure that served as slave quarters built around 1820. Another arcade leads to an early building functioning as a dairy, privy, or garden folly. Covering two acres the house and its dependencies are considered the most comprehensive Georgian town house complex extant in the country.

Colonel Robert Brewton House
71 Church St., Charleston; privately owned

This house is believed to be the oldest surviving "single house" in Charleston dating back to before 1730, thus its National Landmark status recognizing this unique architectural style. The single house design refers to the one room width facing the street stretching up two or three stories, and the entry removed to the center of the long side (two rooms long with center foyer). This long side usually faces south to catch prevailing breezes. Later versions incorporated double piazzas (porches) for shading and additional cooling in the hot, humid climate of semi-tropical Charleston. The floor plan of the single house called for a doorway on the side piazza to enter the porch and then lead to the central doorway of the house. Typically, a living room and a dining room flanked the central foyer on the ground level with a formal drawing room on the street side second level and another room across the hall. A third level contained the bedrooms.

The Robert Brewton House exemplifies the early single house design in other ways as well. It has no below ground basement (Charleston is mostly too low for integrating basements) but extends into a long narrow lot where the kitchen and carriage houses and servants' quarters are close by for utilitarian purposes. It has corner quoining and keystones over the windows with a hip roof. Late 19th-century piazzas were added but removed at a later date, and a modern masonry coating has been applied over the old stucco surface.

Miles Brewton (grandfather of Miles Brewton in the previous listing) came to Charleston in 1684 from Barbados and acquired/may have built the house around 1730. A similar architectural style in the West Indies may have influenced Brewton to embrace the benefits of its "cooling technology." The elder Brewton was a goldsmith and militia officer and gave the house to his son, Robert Brewton (father of the younger Miles Brewton). Robert was also a goldsmith and later followed his

Robert Brewton House, Charleston
Tina E. Mayland

father as Powder Receiver for the city. A 1733 deed shows that Robert's sister, Mrs. Thomas Dale, received the house next door at 73 Church Street from their father too. One hopes it was a good arrangement as the two houses are sited a mere three feet apart. Keeping it all in the family, Robert sold his house in 1745 to another sister, Rebecca, and her husband, Jordan Roche. It later passed out of the family but has been carefully maintained as the earliest extant single house demonstrating this vernacular form in 18th-century Charleston architecture. Hundreds of this style are found all over the peninsula; a very fine later evolution is the Simmons-Edwards House at 14 Legare Street (see below).

Charleston Historic District

Calhoun Street to East Bay/East Battery to Murray Boulevard to Lockwood Boulevard, Charleston; Charleston Visitor Reception and Transportation Center, 375 Meeting St., 800-774-0006; charlestoncvb.com; open daily 8:30 a.m. to 5 p.m. except major holidays

If anything is more remarkable than Charleston's softly pastel colors, cobblestone streets, graceful church spires, and elegant old homes with their exquisite interiors— it has to be the fact that any of it still exists at all. No other colonial city has suffered so many calamities as often as Charleston. Time after time, fire has left vast areas of the city in ashes. The city was bombarded during war twice—once by the British during the Revolution and again by northern cannon in the War Between the States. Mother Nature has repeatedly hurled fierce hurricanes and tornadoes at the city, and it has been cracked and shaken periodically by terrible earthquakes.

And yet, as you walk through the large and little streets south of Calhoun, you find them lined with fascinating architectural relics of the past. It's hard to imagine that much of what looks so timeless and permanent today could so easily have been swept away by any number of man-made disasters or devastating natural happenstances.

After the US Navy Yard military presence was established in 1904, Charleston stepped up to meet the demands of a country heading into two World Wars. As the economy improved so did Charleston's awakening of the historical and cultural treasures still in her possession. A few early visionaries rose to meet the challenge of architectural preservation and restoration. Spurred to action by a threat of demolition to the Joseph Manigault House (1803) and other historic structures in the old city, Susan Pringle Frost (1873–1960) led the movement that formed the

Roadside Marker of Charleston Historic District
Tina E. Mayland

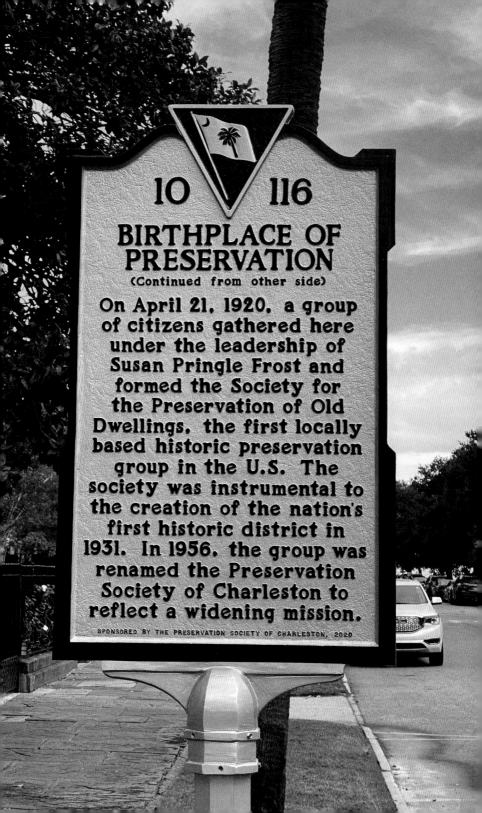

10 116

BIRTHPLACE OF PRESERVATION

(Continued from other side)

On April 21, 1920, a group of citizens gathered here under the leadership of Susan Pringle Frost and formed the Society for the Preservation of Old Dwellings, the first locally based historic preservation group in the U.S. The society was instrumental to the creation of the nation's first historic district in 1931. In 1956, the group was renamed the Preservation Society of Charleston to reflect a widening mission.

SPONSORED BY THE PRESERVATION SOCIETY OF CHARLESTON, 2020

Preservation of Old Dwelling Houses in 1920. Many challenges ensued that tested the mettle of the group resulting in some exciting wins and tragic losses of historic properties. But this groundwork led to legal protection in the form of the nation's first Historic District Zoning Ordinance, adopted in 1931. Now called the Preservation Society of Charleston, the organization along with the Historic Charleston Foundation, established in 1947, continues to keep a watchful eye and vocal presence in the ongoing battle between preservation and modernization, helping to preserve Charleston's treasure trove of historic architecture for future generations.

As a result of these efforts the Charleston Historic District, also known as the Old and Historic District, has a superlative array of 18th- and 19th-century architecture due to its 350-year history of prominence in commercial trade largely through its important eastern seaboard port. A variety of architectural styles emerged during times of prosperity showcasing wealth through high quality structures. One of the most noted forms is the "Charleston single house," which is one room wide, with a central hallway and the narrow end of the house "turned" toward the street, often with two-story side piazzas (or porches) for catching cooling breezes. (See Robert Brewton House in previous listing.) The 502-acre protected area is in the southern tip of peninsular Charleston bounded by the Ashley and Cooper Rivers and the main east-west thoroughfare of Calhoun Street. It has been expanded five times in 1970, 1978, 1984, 1985, and 1986. There are 101 properties and districts listed on the National Register of Historic Places in the city, including 34 National Historic Landmarks.

College of Charleston
66 George St., Charleston; 843-805-5507; cofc.edu; open daily for self-guided tours; free

Recognized as the first municipal college in the United States and the oldest institution of higher learning in South Carolina, the College of Charleston was founded in 1770. The College proudly counts among their founders no less than three signers of the Declaration of Independence (Thomas Heyward Jr., Arthur Middleton, Edward Rutledge) and three framers of the US Constitution (Charles Pinckney, Charles Cotesworth Pinckney, John Rutledge). These men and others recognized the need for a college of higher education in the growing colony of South Carolina.

Three original buildings made up the college for nearly 200 years. The centerpiece of the main campus is Harrison Randolph Hall begun in 1828 and designed by William Strickland of Philadelphia. By 1850 Charleston architect Edward Brickell White added wings to the existing structure with Ionic pilasters supporting curvilinear front gables. He also added a two-story pedimented portico with six imposing

College of Charleston, Charleston
Joe Perry

Ionic columns on an arcaded base; it was flanked with double wrought-iron stair-cases all creating an iconic center façade. The Porter's Lodge, also designed by White, serves as a gateway to the original campus and was built in the 1850s in the Classical Revival style. The first library building now called Towell Library was designed by George E. Walker and completed in 1856. It features two-story arched Italianate style windows, Tuscan pilasters, and corner quoining. Inside, the main room has a large central ceiling medallion and is surrounded by a gallery. All three structures are clad in time-worn stucco and contained within wrought-iron fencing around the one-block site. In 1857 a cistern was built in the middle of the property as a water reservoir for fighting fires prior to a city water system. Later it was grassed over, and today is the site for May commencement and other special events. This thriving academic institution provides a liberal arts education to more than 11,000 under-graduate and graduate students today.

Now more than 100 buildings—from historic structures to high-tech class-rooms—constitute the campus in the heart of historic downtown Charleston largely located within College, George, and Green Streets. Within this setting the college showcases beautiful landscaping with botanical displays for every season. The campus is always open for self-guided tours.

Drayton Hall
3390 Ashley River Rd., Charleston; 843-769-2600; draytonhall.org; open daily; admission charged

Not a tour of a reconstructed working plantation or the collected decorative arts from a bygone era, Drayton Hall offers an adventure in architecture. Yes, architecture and a great deal more. If for no other reason, Drayton Hall should be seen and experienced as the sole survivor of the ugly 1865 rampage by Union troops, who looted and burned nearly every other plantation house along the Ashley River. But there is more to Drayton Hall, as it also stands as a survivor of many other changes, influences, forces, and times.

It was built between 1738 and 1742 as the country seat (primary home) of John Drayton (1716–1779). The house is considered one of the oldest and finest examples of Georgian-Palladian architecture in America. The structure remains almost untouched as an eloquent statement about 18th-century thinking, craftsmanship, technology, and design. It's one of the few sites left in colonial America so pure, unaltered, and uncompromising. Visitors will find the Drayton Hall story—how it all came to pass—interpreted by a small group of professional guides who lead you through 250 years of time, family genealogy, architectural history, and the economic and social realities of the plantation system. The staff has recorded oral histories of the Drayton family as well as the African Americans so strongly associated with the house and its survival.

Drayton Hall, Charleston
iStock

A map is provided to visitors for a self-guided nature walk through the Drayton property including marsh, riverfront, and forest areas. Major portions of the nature trails are wheelchair accessible. This historic site is now owned by the National Trust for Historic Preservation, and it was named a National Historic Landmark in 1960. Admission prices include a professionally guided tour of the historic house and a self-guided tour of the grounds, including the African American cemetery and their interactive Connections program. A written tour in English, French, or German can be purchased.

Exchange and Provost
122 East Bay St., Charleston; 843-727-2165; 888-763-0448; oldexchange.com; open daily; admission charged

A public building has stood on this site at East Bay and Broad Streets since Charles Towne was moved from its original settlement to its present peninsular location in 1680. The early settlers built their court of guard here. They imprisoned pirates and Native Americans in the building's lower level and held their town meetings upstairs in the hall. The British built the present building to create an impressive presence in the bustling colonial port. With its striking Georgian-Palladian architecture, the Exchange surely did just that. Its location on East Bay where Broad Street terminates, secured its dominance in the cityscape as well. It was completed in 1771 and quickly became the social, political, and economic hub of the growing city.

From its steps, the independent colony of South Carolina was publicly declared in March 1776, leading some to call the Old Exchange the birthplace of the state. During the American Revolution under British occupation, the building was converted to a military prison, where signers of the Declaration of Independence were held in harsh confinement. In 1788 the convention to ratify the US Constitution met in the Old Exchange as leading South Carolinians discussed, debated, and

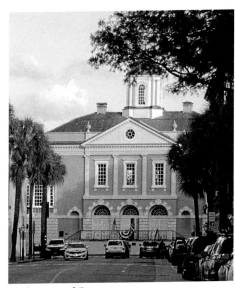

Exchange and Provost
Tina E. Mayland

approved the founding document. Currently, it is one of only four buildings still standing around the country where ratification took place. President George Washington was lavishly entertained here at concerts, dances, and dinners during his 1791 southern tour. From 1815 to 1896, the building served both the Federal and Confederate governments as the Charleston post office. It was also the site of numerous public slave auctions held prior to Emancipation. In 1913 Congress deeded the building to the Daughters of the American Revolution of South Carolina. During an excavation of the dungeon in 1965, part of the original 1701 seawall of Charles Towne was discovered. The Half-Moon Battery is the only part of the old city wall that is accessible for viewing by the public. Today, the Old Exchange and Provost Dungeon is still owned by the DAR and is operated by the City of Charleston as a museum and event venue.

Farmers' and Exchange Bank
141 East Bay St., Charleston; privately owned

Among Charleston's traditional architecture landscape, the Farmers' and Exchange Bank stands out. Its Moorish Revival style is a bold and distinctive exception. The bank was designed by Charleston architect Francis D. Lee who described it as "Sarcenic" and one that possibly gave him a challenge, if not an enjoyable change from his usual pursuits. Moorish architecture depictions in Washington Irving's *The Alhambra: A Series of Tales and Sketches of the Moors and Spaniards* published in 1832 and revised in 1851 may have influenced the design. It was completed in 1854 as Charleston's financial district was expanding above Broad Street along East Bay. It was a departure from the conservative norm of the other banking institutions and must have garnered a lot of attention at the time, perhaps just what the Farmers' and Exchange Bank board hoped.

The street front façade of the two-story building is clad in pale New Jersey sandstone and darker red Connecticut stone in a striping pattern. It is three bays wide, displaying numerous eastern-inspired decorative features. The first-floor triple entries are intricately carved, separated by striped Moorish pilasters, and topped with circular windows outlined with curved sandstone blocks. The second-floor windows are tall and capped with horseshoe arches with scalloped edges. (These are said to be reminiscent of the Alcazar at Seville and the Mosque at Cordoba.) The large cornice above uses muquarnas, or honeycomb vaulting common in Islamic architecture, to crown the edifice.

The interior reflects the eclecticism and exuberance of the exterior façade. A vestibule leads to the original two-story counting room, which is fifty feet long,

Farmers' and Exchange Bank, Charleston
Tina E. Mayland

twenty-one feet wide with a coffered ceiling and skylight. Arcaded walls and ornate plasterwork continue the fanciful design. It was made a National Historic Landmark in 1973 as a foremost example of Moorish Revival picturesque style in American architecture.

Fireproof Building
100 Meeting St., Charleston; 843-723-3225; schistory.org; open Tues through Sat; admission charged

Originally called the Charleston District Record Building when it was constructed 1822–27, it is now known as the Fireproof Building. Always concerned with fires (and Charleston had experienced three devastating ones by this date), the city commissioned Charleston architect Robert Mills (who later designed the Washington Monument and the US Treasury Building) to design a structure that would withstand the spread of fire. He substituted non-combustible materials like brick, brownstone, and stucco on the exterior; window casings were made of cast iron, and a central cupola illuminated the cantilevered stone staircases inside as no other illumination was allowed in this time prior to electricity. Mills's choice of materials he said were "to render the building secure from fire," and it is recognized as the first fireproof building in America. The onsite construction manager, John Spidle, made some changes to Mills's original plans, but the building is an impressive one, sitting on the northwest corner of Washington Park at Meeting and Chalmers Streets. It is designed in a simple Greek Revival style with little decoration other than the Doric-columned porticoes in front and back.

When the County of Charleston was created, the building housed county records and served as coroner and tax offices for over a hundred years. Since 1943 it is home to the South Carolina Historical Society (founded in 1855), who maintains one of the most important private historic document collections in the country. The Society served as a repository and archive for scholarly study and in-depth examination of original South Carolina material. As their collection outgrew the space, the Historical Society shifted gears to offer a new approach. They sent much of their collection to the College of Charleston's Addlestone Library where it is more accessible for researchers.

The Society then took on a major renovation that was completed in 2017 to update all the systems in the Fireproof Building for a secure and climate-controlled environment for the rest of their collection; the renovation incorporated an event venue as well as a museum space dedicated to tell the state's history through interactive exhibits and primary materials from the perspective of some of the early historical figures who lived through it, such as local Native American Cassique of Kiawah, and colonial-era indigo pioneer Eliza Lucas Pinckney. The museum also pays tribute

Fireproof Building, Charleston
Tina E. Mayland

to Robert Mills and the Fireproof Building itself. SCHS now welcomes the public here to share its collection with a much broader audience.

William Gibbes House
64 South Battery, Charleston; privately owned

Picture this home as it was originally sited facing the Ashley River and the 300-foot wharf William Gibbes owned, generating his wealth in colonial Charleston. It must have appeared quite grand to approaching boats. Now its river view is obstructed by many residential homes, but in Gibbes's day he could look out from his front doorstep to his waterfront commercial complex of warehouses, stores, and a coffeehouse. He was one of Charleston's wealthiest planter-merchants at the time and built his Georgian home c. 1772 as a wood frame (black cypress) "double house" with four rooms on each floor, divided two and two by a central hall. It is set on a high stone foundation with double flanking staircases leading to the entry landing. The façade is five bays wide with pedimented first floor windows and bracketed sills. Most impressive is the attic-level gabled pediment with its acanthus leaf carved console brackets and embellished trim; the front entryway repeats this elaborate pediment on a smaller scale supported by four pilasters on either side of the door and lovely sidelight windows.

William Gibbes House, Charleston
Tina E. Mayland

Unfortunately, Gibbes was unable to enjoy his property undisturbed. The British occupation of Charleston in 1780 interceded, and he was imprisoned along with other Charleston patriots and his family evicted from their home. The British army took over the large, spacious house for a hospital until they left Charleston in 1782. After the war ended Gibbes and his family returned to their home, and he lived there until his death in 1789. Sarah Moore Smith purchased the property in 1794 and is responsible for much of the interior redecoration. She favored the more graceful Adamesque style featuring delicately carved doorway and fireplace surrounds, mantels, and plaster ceilings. The dramatic third floor ballroom (20' x 34') with its coved ceiling, plaster medallion, and corner fan decorations add to the grandeur of the house. Of other historical interest is that Mrs. Smith was the grandmother of Charleston's Grimké sisters, Angelina and Sarah, abolitionists and women's rights advocates in the Civil War era.

More alterations to the property were made by Cornelia Roebling, daughter-in-law of the designer of the Brooklyn Bridge, Washington A. Roebling, after her purchase in 1928. She installed an 18th-century chinoiserie style room inside and hired noted landscape designer Loutrel Briggs to restore and augment the gardens on the nearly one-acre property. In keeping with the popular Colonial Revival style, the garden features an allée and a reflecting pool with a fountain. Other earlier features were retained such as the brick wall with stuccoed arches surrounding the lot, a brick privy, and kitchen house. The carriage house and stables were converted to garages with servants' rooms above while keeping their original brick and tabby exterior and tile roofs.

The William Gibbes House is considered one of the country's finest classical Georgian town homes and exemplifies careful evolution of a very fine 18th-century architectural gem over the centuries.

Edwin DuBose Heyward House
76 Church St., Charleston; privately owned

Charleston's own Edwin DuBose Heyward (1885–1940) wrote the legendary 1925 novel here, which inspired a renaissance of artistic effort in and about the city and its people. The story is based on the life of a poor, crippled black street vendor and his tragic love for an abused, drug-addicted woman.

The novelist's playwright wife, Dorothy, co-wrote the successful stage play that opened on Broadway in 1927. None other than George Gershwin felt *Porgy* was just the vehicle he was looking for to create a new art form: the American folk opera. The world-famous work known as *Porgy and Bess* was produced by New York's Theatre Guild in 1935, brightening the darkest days of the Depression. Since then, millions of music lovers all over the world have thrilled to Gershwin's classic American opera, *Porgy and Bess*. So mainstream now are the music and lyrics to "Summertime" and "I've Got Plenty of Nothin'" that many fans don't realize the opera was based on the book penned by Charlestonian Edwin DuBose Heyward.

"Cabbage Row" at nearby 89-91 Church Street is the inspirational setting of the story and took its name from the vegetables regularly sold from carts and windowsills by the area's black residents. Heyward named it "Catfish Row" in the book, so today a hanging sign designates it as such. Now, this section houses quaint little shops, but anyone familiar with the story will readily see that this place and the alleys around and behind it could easily have been the novel's original scene. Was the story based on truth? Was there ever a

Edwin DuBose Heyward House
Courtesy of Library of Congress

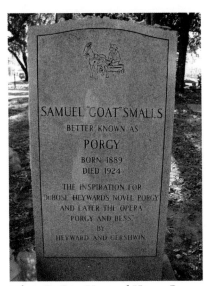

Edwin DuBose Heyward House–Porgy Grave
Lee Davis Perry

crippled vendor named Porgy who won, then lost, the love of a troubled woman named Bess? Many older Charlestonians tell of a poor, crippled man who lived here in the early 1920s and used a small goat cart to get around. His name was Samuel Smalls. More avid music lovers and Porgy fans may want to visit Smalls's grave, which is well marked in the churchyard of James Island Presbyterian Church at 1632 Fort Johnson Rd., the intersection of Folly and Fort Johnson Roads. Look for the marker to Porgy beside the parking area just outside the fenced churchyard.

The house at 76 Church was designated a National Historic Landmark in 1971 because it was where Heyward wrote the book *Porgy*. It dates from c. 1785 and features brick covered with early stucco and a clay pantile roof. In recent years it was combined with 78 Church Street making one residence.

Heyward-Washington House
87 Church St., Charleston; 843-722-2996; charlestonmuseum.org; open daily year-round for guided tours; admission charged

This handsome, early Charleston "dwelling house" is known by two names because of two prominent Americans associated with it—one an owner, the other a distinguished guest. It was built in 1772 by Daniel Heyward, a wealthy rice planter and the father of Thomas Heyward Jr., a South Carolina signer of the Declaration of Independence. It is documented that the younger Heyward lived in the house until 1794. In 1791 President George Washington made a grand tour of the new nation and included Charleston on his itinerary. In anticipation of this distinguished visitor, the city rented Heyward's house for Washington's accommodations, and Heyward was thus displaced to his country house for the duration. In Washington's diary, he recorded his visit to the property, saying, "The lodgings provided for me in this place were very good, being the furnished house of a gentleman at present residing in the country; but occupied by a person placed there on purpose to accommodate me."

Today the house is furnished with a magnificent collection of period antiques, especially some fine Charleston-made furniture of the 18th century. Look for the

Heyward-Washington House
Courtesy of The Charleston Museum, Charleston, South Carolina

famous Holmes bookcase that still bears the scars of an incoming British mortar from the days of the American Revolution. This is the only 18th-century house museum in the city with original outbuildings (kitchen, carriage house, and "necessary") still a part of the courtyard. There's also find a small formal garden with plantings in keeping with the period of the house. Heyward-Washington House was saved from destruction in the early 1920s by the Preservation Society of Charleston. It is now a National Historic Landmark (1970) owned and operated by the Charleston Museum. Note that the Charleston Museum offers discounted combination ticket prices for the museum, this house, and the Joseph Manigault House (see below).

Hibernian Hall
105 Meeting St., Charleston; privately owned; limited access

Considered one of the most significant examples of Greek Revival architecture in Charleston, Hibernian Hall is the result of the Hibernian Society's national competition for submission of plans for a meeting hall in the early 1830s. The Society, founded in 1801, was created as a social and charitable organization to provide aid to Irish immigrant families. Having acquired a site on Meeting Street nearly opposite

Hibernian Hall, Charleston
Tina E. Mayland

Robert Mills's Fireproof Building (see above) in the same Greek Revival style, plans were drawn up by Philadelphia architect Thomas U. Walter (later designer of the enlargement of the US Capitol dome in Washington, DC) who was paid $100 for his work in 1833. But construction of the building was delayed several times. One problem was internal disagreement on whether the building should contain a meeting hall and a hotel (generating revenue for its charitable endeavors) or merely a meeting hall. Another factor was escalating construction costs in part due to the great fire of 1838 damaging nearly one-third of the city and driving up costs for materials and labor. Eventually construction began in 1839 and was completed in early 1841 at a cost of $40,000. When Hibernian Hall was opened, music, dancing, and toasts were raised extolling it as "a monument to future generations of the public spirit and liberality of the sons of Hibernia" and adding to Charleston's resurgence of commercial and civic structures "rising from her ashes more solid and beautiful than ever, soon will the remembrance of her late misfortune

Hibernian Hall, Charleston
Tina E. Mayland

be buried in oblivion, may her people never falter or flag, until she is crowned 'the Queen of the South.'"

Walter's plan was based on the Ionic Temple on the Ilissus in Athens, Greece, and met the building committee's request of a simple, classical design—one exception being the gilded Irish harp in relief over the door. The two-story building is brick (not the more expensive granite specified by Walter) covered in stucco painted white. It is enclosed with a wrought-iron fence and cast-iron gas lanterns. In another nod to its Irish connections, a piece of the Giant's Causeway in County Antrim, Northern Ireland, was placed on the portico in 1851. The grand Ionic hexastyle portico collapsed in the earthquake of 1886. It was rebuilt with some modifications including changing the proportions of the columns, more ornate cornice modillions, and an Italianate window in the pediment. The elegant interior departs from the simplicity of the exterior and remains largely unchanged; the vestibule features a three-story rotunda with staircases leading to circular columned balconies ultimately reaching up to a coffered dome with an oculus.

Hibernian Hall has served its purpose well as the site for innumerable Hibernian Society functions such as their annual St. Patrick's Day banquet; it also hosts the January Ball of the St. Cecilia Society, Charleston's oldest and most exclusive social event. It served as the headquarters for Stephen A. Douglas's nomination as a Democratic candidate (one of three) opposing Lincoln in the 1860 election. The

Society's membership has expanded to both Protestant and Catholic, not necessarily of Irish ancestry. Often it is the venue for wedding receptions and other large festivities.

Huguenot Church
136 Church St., Charleston; 843-722-4385; huguenot-church.org; open daily, limited hours; free

French Protestants, or Huguenots, were followers of the 16th-century French reformer John Calvin. They received harsh treatment by the reining French Catholic court, and, after King Louis XIV revoked the Edict of Nantes (1685) protecting their rights, there was an enormous flight away from France by Protestants. Many of them came to the Carolinas. The Huguenot Church in Charleston was organized in 1681, and groups of believers arrived in this area between 1680 and 1763. In 1706 the Church Act established the Anglican Church as the official religion in South Carolina, and, slowly, most Huguenot churches were absorbed into what became Episcopal congregations. The Huguenot Church in Charleston is the outstanding exception; it is the only remaining independent Huguenot congregation in America.

The original church building was erected in 1687 but was destroyed in 1796 due to fire. A replacement was finished in 1800 but torn down in 1844 to make way for a new structure. This church was the city's first to be built (1845) in the Gothic Revival style. It was designed by Edward Brickell White, a noted Charleston architect who is credited with popularizing the Gothic style in America. The church was damaged by shelling during the Civil War and nearly demolished by the 1886 earthquake. Each time, it was painstakingly restored. The church obtained National Historic Landmark status in 1973, and the building underwent a major refurbishing in 1997.

Huguenot Church, Charleston
Tina E. Mayland

Huguenot Church, Charleston
Shutterstock

The church's famous Tracker organ, restored in 1967 by the Preservation Society of Charleston and the Charleston chapter of the American Organists Guild, is one of the city's true musical treasures. It was built by the famed American organ builder Henry Erben, and is carved to resemble a Gothic chapel. Its tone is similar to the Baroque organs of Handel's and Bach's time. It is truly one of the last of its kind anywhere in the country. Regular Sunday services are held; but now, only once a year, a service is conducted in French.

Kahal Kadosh Beth Elohim
90 Hasell St., Charleston; 843-723-1090; kkbe.org; open Mon through Thurs, Sun for tours; donation suggested

People of the Jewish faith have lived in South Carolina for more than 300 years. The provisions for religious tolerance offered by Carolina's Fundamental Constitution were unique for the time, and news of the friendly environment spread across Europe and the West Indies. Most of Carolina's early Jews were people of Sephardic heritage whose ancestors had been expelled from Spain and Portugal centuries earlier.

Over 100 years before the Civil War, hundreds of Jewish immigrants came to South Carolina from Prussia and Poland. They were attracted to the Charleston area by the busy port, by the already established Jewish community and synagogues,

Kahal Kadosh Beth Elohim, Charleston
Courtesy Library of Congress

Kahal Kadosh Beth Elohim, Charleston
Tina E. Mayland

and by the opening of the back country to settlers. Early settlers opened dry-goods stores and became doctors, lawyers, journalists, and soldiers. As time passed, they ran the stores that were the very center of the community. Here is part of Jewish Reformer Isaac Harby's letter to Secretary of State James Monroe in 1816: "Jews are by no means to be considered as a religious sect, tolerated by the government: they constitute a portion of the People . . . Quakers and Catholics; Episcopalians and Presbyterians, Baptists and Jews, all constitute one great political family."

The congregation of Kahal Kadosh Beth Elohim was organized in 1749. It is the oldest synagogue in continuous use in the United States. According to synagogue records, it is also the longest surviving Reform synagogue in the world. Beth Elohim is acknowledged as the birthplace of Reform Judaism in the United States, tracing its origins back to 1824. This is a branch of Judaism that places more emphasis on traditional religious and moral values, instead of rigid ceremonial and ritualistic detail. The present 1840 Greek Revival structure was designed by Cyrus L. Warner, and it was made a National Historic Landmark in 1980. The graceful but massive wrought-iron fence that faces Hasell Street dates to the original 1794 synagogue. Rabbi Gustavus Pozanski, consecrating Kahal Kadosh Beth Elohim's new building in 1841, said, "This synagogue is our temple, this city our Jerusalem, this happy land our Palestine."

Laffey (USS)
40 Patriots Point Rd., Mt. Pleasant; 843-884-2727, 866-831-1720; www.patriotspoint.org; open daily year-round; parking fee and admission charged

Patriots Point Naval and Maritime Museum is the name given to a huge maritime museum complex seen as you cross the Arthur Ravenel Jr. Bridge over the Cooper River from Charleston to Mt. Pleasant. It consists mainly of two World War II era in-situ ships (permanently situated): a destroyer, USS *Laffey*, and the flagship of the museum, USS *Yorktown* (aircraft carrier). Other exhibits in the complex are the true-to-scale Vietnam War Naval Support Base, the Cold War Submarine Memorial, and the Medal of Honor Museum.

The heroic destroyer *Laffey* (DD-724) was named for the previous Laffey (DD-459) that was sunk during the battle for Guadalcanal on November 13, 1942. The Laffey name itself was in honor of Civil War Medal of Honor recipient Seaman Bartlett Laffey. USS *Laffey* was commissioned on February 8, 1944, and it participated in the giant D-Day landings of Allied troops at Normandy four months later. Next *Laffey* was transferred to the Pacific in support of the US offensive against Japan. During just one hour on April 16, 1945, off Okinawa she was struck by five Japanese kamikaze suicide planes and hit by three bombs. The *Laffey's* gallant crew, reduced by a third due to death and injury, not only kept the heavily damaged ship afloat but also managed to shoot down 11 planes during the attack.

After World War II, the *Laffey* served during the Korean War as a part of the lengthy naval bombardment of Wonsan Harbor in 1952, and then in the Atlantic Fleet until she was decommissioned in 1975. Dubbed "The Ship That Would Not Die," USS *Laffey* (DD-724) is the most decorated WWII era US destroyer still in existence. She joined the Patriots Point fleet in 1981 and was made a National Historic Landmark as well as the *Yorktown* five years later. A tour route on the *Laffey* lets

USS Laffey

Department of Defense (The appearance of US Department of Defense [DoD] visual information does not imply or constitute DoD endorsement.)

you see the bridge, battle stations, living quarters, and various displays of destroyer activities.

Joseph Manigault House
**350 Meeting St., Charleston; 843-723-2996; charlestonmuseum
.org; open daily year-round; admission charged**

At the beginning of the 19th century, Charleston architecture was still very much dominated by what was fashionable in Mother England. This house, designed and built in 1803 by Charleston gentleman-architect Gabriel Manigault for his brother Joseph, was certainly no exception. Today it remains one of America's most beautiful examples of the graceful Adam style. Descendants of French Huguenots who emigrated to Charleston fleeing religious persecution in Europe, the Manigault family acquired land and prospered, rising to become one of the leading families in the state. Both Manigault brothers were wealthy rice planters with sophisticated tastes.

Joseph Manigault House, Charleston
Courtesy of The Charleston Museum, Charleston, South Carolina

Gabriel had studied in Geneva and London, where the Adam influence was at its height, and he maintained an extensive architectural library of his own.

The impressive home is constructed of locally made brown brick rising three stories high over a tall basement. Curvilinear bays face the north and east sides with double-tiered piazzas on the west and south sides. Upon entering the large central hall, the house is distinguished by one of the most graceful, curved staircases in the city leading up to elegant second-floor drawing and withdrawing rooms. The house displays an outstanding collection of Charleston, American, English, and French furniture of the Federal period. Original color schemes are presented in many of the spaces.

Don't miss the charming gate temple in the rear garden. During the 1920s, when the Manigault House was very nearly torn down in the name of progress, Gabriel Manigault's classical gate temple was used as the restroom for an oil company's service station, then on the garden site. The property became a rallying point for Susan Pringle Frost founding the Society for the Preservation of Old Dwellings to save it. Later, during World War II, the house served as a USO canteen for servicemen passing through Charleston's busy Navy Yard en route to battle stations overseas. Today it is a National Historic Landmark (1973) owned and operated by the Charleston Museum. The Garden Club of Charleston, guided by an 1820 watercolor rendered by Charlotte Manigault, restored the parterre garden and continues to help maintain it. A work yard composed of a kitchen, slave quarters, and other dependencies now gone are delineated with interpretive signage. Combination tickets for adults, which include admission for the Charleston Museum and Heyward-Washington House (see above) are available for two sites or for all three.

Market Hall and Sheds
188 Meeting St., Charleston; 843-937-0920; thecharlestoncity market.com; open daily year-round; free; Museum at Market Hall; 843-723-1541; museumatmarkethall.com; Tues through Sat, 10 a.m. to 4 p.m.; admission charged

The historic Charleston City Market (1804) is one of the most colorful and popular tourist destinations in the city. The Market's shopping area is flanked by busy, one-way streets (called North and South Market Streets), and Meeting and East Bay Streets. The Market may be one of the oldest "shopping malls" in the United States. It was built on land that Charles Cotesworth Pinckney, who was a signer of the US Constitution, ceded to the city in the 18th century for use as a public market in perpetuity. Originally it was designated as a centralized marketplace for the fish, meat, vegetables, and wares brought in from the nearby wharves and the growing fields outside the colonial city.

Before the advent of refrigeration, the meat butchering and fish cleaning was done onsite, and the gutters of Market Street were fouled with the trimmings and inedible refuse from each day's knifework. The Market became a smelly and unsanitary eyesore in the heart of the city. But to the rescue came Mother Nature's feathered sanitary crew, the less than handsome turkey buzzard, euphemistically described in polite society as "Charleston Eagles." At the height of the Market's output, the sky over the area darkened with the circling scavengers waiting for another shovel-load of entrails and fish heads. Mercifully, those days are gone, and tourism transformed the space into a merchandise market for gift and souvenir shopping.

The Great Hall (1841) is an imposing one-story building in the Greek Revival style fronting Meeting Street and easily recognized with its colorful brownstone stucco façade, red sandstone detail, and green ironwork. Its design is based on the Temple of the Wingless Victory (Athena Nike) on the Acropolis in Athens, Greece. The building served as a former recruiting station for Confederate soldiers during the Civil War, and a small museum of Confederate relics has operated here since 1899 by the United Daughters of the Confederacy. The Hall sits atop the sky-lit, ground-level arcade that stretches from Meeting to Church Streets covering 18,300 square feet of corridor. A multi-year $5.5 million renovation completed in 2011 houses a string of new specialty shops, boutiques, and eateries. The three open-air sheds continue to offer a variety of goods as they have done for more than two centuries. Made up of low brick buildings, these sheds have survived hurricanes, earthquakes, tornadoes, fires, and even Civil War bombardment. Here, vendors of all types rent

Market Hall and Sheds, Charleston
Tina E. Mayland

spaces and booths to hawk their wares including many of the local sweetgrass basket makers. The Market is a must-see for every Charleston visitor, and its magic seems to lie in its eternal spontaneity. It's an ever-changing kaleidoscope of things and smells (better ones now) and sounds and people who all seem to be in a carnival mood. It's different every day, and it's always the same.

Middleton Place
4300 Ashley River Rd., Charleston; 843-556-6020, 800-782-3608; open daily year-round; admission charged

Middleton Place, site of America's oldest landscaped garden, is one of the Lowcountry's most famous plantations and another National Historic Landmark along the banks of the rich and fascinating Ashley River. This was the home of Henry Middleton, president of the First Continental Congress, and his son Arthur, a signer of the Declaration of Independence. The sheer size and scope of Middleton's gardens tell a great deal about the man and his grand vision. The 12-acre greensward, with its grazing sheep and strutting peacocks, creates an unforgettable image for the first-time visitor. Not to be missed is the view of the Ashley River from the high terraces of the azalea, camellia, and rose gardens. The green grass ripples down the hillside to the graceful butterfly lakes below.

This bucolic, pastoral scene belies the frenzy of activity and the vast labor force needed to maintain this busy world. On the Middleton Place grounds is Eliza's House, an actual freedman's dwelling furnished as it was in the 1870s when it was lived in by freed people who stayed on the plantation after the emancipation. At the lively plantation stableyards, with active displays of day-to-day life, you'll find a blacksmith, a potter, weavers, and carpenters all busy at work and eager to explain and demonstrate their skills. The main house, built sometime before 1741,

Middleton Place, Charleston
Shutterstock

Middleton Place Statuary
Tina E. Mayland

was—like neighboring Magnolia Plantation's—burned in 1865 by Union troops. As the story goes, the soldiers drank wine and had a glorious dinner with heavy silver and fancy linen at the main house, then they set fire to it and left. The south flanker building (added about 1755) was least damaged by the fire, and it was essentially rebuilt in the early years of the 20th century in its present form.

The restaurant at Middleton Place serves authentic Lowcountry cuisine for lunch daily and dinner on weekends. Just past the rice mill, a path leads into the forest and up a hill to the Middleton Inn, a 55-room riverside oasis for discerning travelers. With vine-covered stucco and unblinking modern glass walls, it is a contemporary structure with a nod to its inspirational 18th-century setting at Middleton Place.

Mulberry Plantation
1904 N. Mulberry Dr., Moncks Corner; privately owned

Mulberry Plantation, or Mulberry Castle as it was once called, inspires a leap to the past on many levels. As orderly and stately as it appears, it was located in the raw frontier occupied by Native Americans who had a camp on the high bluff where the house sits only a few years earlier. It sheltered Yemassee Indian War (1715–1716) colonial refugees, and two small cannons of the period were later excavated there in 1835. It served as a military headquarters of a cavalry unit during the Revolutionary War. But it was built foremost as an impressive home by a man seeking his fortune in the Carolina Lowcountry.

The property was originally part of a land grant to Sir Peter Colleton whose son exchanged it with Thomas Broughton. Broughton had a diverse career of Indian trader, soldier, planter, and politician. He was married to the daughter of Sir Nathaniel Johnson, formerly governor of Antigua and South Carolina. Broughton, too, later served as royal governor of South Carolina province from 1735 until his death in 1737. The house he built was no doubt intended to make a statement and creatively blended several styles of architecture into one unique, cohesive plan. Influences of

Mulbery Plantation, Moncks Corner
Chip Hall, Plantation Services

the old-world style of the 17th-century Jacobean period from the English country-side, and French and Anglo-Dutch baroque features can all be found here. It was built in 1714 (some say a bit earlier in 1711); the iron weathervanes topping the four corner towers display "1714" numerals under royal crowns, which seem to confirm the completion date.

The main body of the two-story house is brick laid in the English bond pattern. Dormer windows pierce the jerkinhead (clipped ends) gambrel roof along with two chimneys providing the Georgian symmetry to its façade. It strays a bit from this symmetry on the inside with no central hallway but direct entry into the front parlor and a stairwell hallway removed to the rear. Redecorated around 1800 the first-floor staircase, cornices, and mantels were modified to the more refined, formal Adam-esque style. Upstairs the panels and molding of the doors and mantels retain their original 18th-century woodwork.

The most unusual feature is the four one-story towers attached to each corner of the house with their bell-shaped turret roofs; these, especially, give the fortress appearance to the Castle and may in fact have had trap doors for storing gun powder in its early days. Another interesting feature is the wood carving in the pediment over the entrance porch. It depicts a fruited mulberry branch framed by a horseshoe. Lore says a large mulberry tree was growing wild on the site and perhaps also refers to Broughton's desire (with good luck) to cultivate silk for commercial production just as his father-in-law's plantation, Silk Hope, was doing. In fact, rice, not silk, became the major crop at Mulberry with its extensive rice fields stretching out from the high

Mulbery Plantation, Moncks Corner
Chip Hall, Plantation Services

bluff of the home site into a western branch of the Cooper River. A fortress perhaps, but unmistakably one of the most distinctive 18th-century plantation houses
in America.

Old Marine Hospital
20 Franklin St., Charleston; limited access

The city's first Gothic Revival structure was designed by architect Robert Mills, a
Charleston native. The Old Marine Hospital had its beginnings much earlier in the
federal act of 1749, which provided for "a public hospital for all sick sailors and other
transient persons." Eventually in 1830 funds were appropriated by Congress to hire
Mills who was working in Baltimore on other federal buildings. Work began about
1831 and was finished in 1833. The busy port city of Charleston imposed a fee on
visiting ships, and, jointly with the federal government's monetary support, the hospital began operations in 1834.

The two-story, rectangular masonry building has a hip roof and a raised basement with arcaded arches typical of Mills's designs. The prominent architectural feature is the two-tiered porch with its opposing entrance bays rising all the way to the
pointed Gothic arches at the roof line. To reach the interior from the bays there is
a central doorway flanked by tall Gothic windows, and the motif is repeated in the
iron porch railings and quatrefoil-shaped columns. Slightly reminiscent of medieval

monasteries, Mills used similar plans around the country that reflected the popular sentiment that this style was appropriate for a hospital environment.

The patients were cared for in eight wards and "took air" on the porches. At the beginning of the Civil War, Alexander N. Talley, medical director of Confederate forces in South Carolina, oversaw the hospital serving ill and wounded soldiers, but any ill seamen were still permitted admission. The building sustained such extensive damage from Union bombardment that after the war, the federal government decided not to continue its operations there. Next, the Episcopal Church held a free school for black children in the former hospital employing local white women as the staff from 1866 to 1870.

Perhaps the Old Marine Hospital is most remembered as the home of the Jenkins Orphanage started by Reverend Daniel Jenkins, a black Baptist minister in 1891. He founded it as an orphanage for African American children and encouraged musical talent he found among them. This evolved into a band that served not only as motivator for the homeless boys, but also a much needed fund-raiser for the orphanage. The Jenkins Orphanage Band started out performing on the streets of Charleston to the delight of the locals and tourists alike who passed a hat for donations. Some members would also dance to their jazzy music and are credited with developing the "The Charleston," a dance craze that became popular all around

Old Marine Hospital, Charleston
Tina E. Mayland

Old Marine Hospital, Charleston
Tina E. Mayland

the world by the 1920s. Over time the band garnered an international reputation abroad, and several members went on to play in the famous orchestras of luminaries like Count Basie, Louis Armstrong, and Duke Ellington.

Currently occupied by the Charleston Housing Authority, the Old Marine Hospital has limited public access.

Parish House of the Circular Congregational Church

150 Meeting St., Charleston; (843) 577-6400; circularchurch.org; grounds and graveyard open year-round; limited access

Circular Congregational Church (1891–1892) was originally called the Independent Church of Charles Towne and was established in 1681 by some of the first

Parish House of the Circular Congregational Church, Charleston
Tina E. Mayland

Parish House of the Circular Congregational Church, Charleston
Tina E. Mayland

settlers. It was one of the first two congregations created in the settlement (the other being St. Philip's Church). The original building was of white brick and was known by locals as the White Meeting House. It is from this early euphemism that Meeting Street, a major thoroughfare in downtown Charleston, takes its name. That building was outgrown and replaced c. 1806 by the first "Circular Church," an impressive structure designed in the Pantheon style by Charleston's famous architect Robert Mills. It is said to have seated 2,000 people, both black and white. The great fire of 1861 swept across the city and took this building with it. The ruins stood mutely until the earthquake of 1886 turned them to rubble. A third (and the present) building on this site was completed in 1892 and is circular in form but Romanesque in style.

The Parish House also designed by Mills was built just prior to the construction of the first Circular Church, and services were held there before the church was completed. It is architecturally significant of Mills's ability to create a Greek Revival temple design on a smaller, well-proportioned scale without diminishing its stately appearance. Located just behind the church among the gravesites and next to neighboring St. Philip's Church graveyard, the elegant, sophisticated structure has one story elevated by a lower arcade. Four Tuscan columns support the entablature and pediment of the portico. Front-facing double staircases with wrought-iron railings lead to a central landing to the large arched, double-door entry. Altogether a proper and splendid structure adding to Robert Mills's architectural legacy across Charleston and beyond.

The church's graveyard is the city's oldest, with monuments dating from 1695. This is the burial ground of Nathaniel Russell. (See Nathaniel Russell House below.) Visitors are welcome to explore the grounds and graveyard. Contact the office for visiting the church at times other than during services.

Pompion Hill Chapel
Pompion Hill Lane, Huger; privately owned with very limited access

It is hard to say what is more captivating—the picturesque bluff of this eastern branch of the Cooper River or the beautiful little chapel built beside it. Surely the combination is an arresting sight in this "back river" location some thirty miles outside of Charleston.

For almost 300 years Pompion Hill Chapel (pronounced "Punkin" locally) has been a place of worship serving the St. Thomas's and St. Denis's parishes near Huger, South Carolina. In 1703 Huguenot planters chose a bluff called Ponkin Hill on the Cooper River branch for their small cypress church. It would be easily accessible by water, the preferred way of travel from the outlying plantations. It was funded by the area's wealthy landowners and Sir Nathaniel Johnson, governor from 1703–1709. With the Church Act of 1706, more financial support came from the Church of England to maintain their chapel of ease (small church built to bring the gospel to outlying areas making it "easy" for planters and their families to attend). Over time the wooden, 30-foot square Ponkin Hill Church deteriorated, but was later replaced by the current chapel near the same site. Reverend Alexander Garden wrote that the

Pompion Hill Chapel, Huger
Tina E. Mayland

sixty-year-old chapel had "become ruinous" and "was too small to accommodate the congregation," thus a new larger brick chapel was built in 1763 measuring 48 by 35 feet.

The result is often called "a miniature Georgian masterpiece," and it is considered one of the finest surviving examples of Anglican parish buildings in the Carolina Lowcountry. It is believed to have been designed by Zachariah Villepontoux who supplied the fine quality brick manufactured on his nearby property, Parnassus Plantation, just as he had previously supplied the brick for St. Michael's Church in Charleston. He even left his mark for posterity by carving his initials "ZV" and the date "1763" in the brick near the north and south doors. Doubtless many enslaved Africans contributed their skills to the structure too. The rectangular structure has a high-pitched, slate jerkinhead (flattened gable) roof; the repetition of the matching arched windows and the symmetry of the Palladian window on the eastern end contribute to the balance and elegance of the Georgian style.

On the inside the focal point is the extraordinary, native red cedar pulpit based on the one in St. Michael's and created by William Axson Jr., a Charleston master carpenter. Steps lead up to the canopied hexagonal pulpit, decorated with egg-and-dart molding, detailed leaf designs, and ecclesiastical inlaid sunburst patterns. Fluted Corinthian columns support the canopy, which is topped by a dove in flight symbolizing the Holy Spirit. Opposite the pulpit is the balustrade-enclosed, rounded chancel illuminated by the Palladian window. Axson, too, carved his name along with a Masonic emblem in a brick near the north door, and who would blame him for wanting to be remembered for his exquisite work here. The backdrop to all these sophisticated features are white plaster walls, a cove tray ceiling, and a red tile floor given by Gabriel Manigault (see Joseph Manigault House above). A bit unusual is the layout of the pews paralleling the long walls facing each other across the center aisle with the liturgical proceedings at the chancel and pulpit to the right and to the left.

Even though the tides have washed away some of the bank and possibly some graves over the centuries, the churchyard tombstones record the names of many important early South Carolinians resting peacefully in the reverence and serenity of

Pompion Hill Chapel, Huger
Tina E. Mayland

the spot. The Pompion Hill Chapel Foundation Inc. provides for the maintenance and preservation and can be reached at 109½ Church St., Charleston, SC 29401.

Powder Magazine
79 Cumberland St., Charleston; 843-722-9350; powdermag.org; open daily year-round; admission charged

Only a couple of blocks from the bustling market area is the oldest public building in the Carolinas. The utilitarian Powder Magazine (1713) predates Charleston's legendary aesthetics. It was built for a time when the still-new English settlement was predominantly interested in self-defense and basic survival. In the early years of the 18th century, Charles Towne was still threatened by Spanish forces, hostile Native Americans, rowdy packs of buccaneers, and an occasional French attack. It was still a walled city, fortified against surprise attack. In August 1702, a survey of the armament in Charles Towne reported "2,306 lbs. of gunpowder, 496 shot of all kind, 28 great guns, 47 Grenada guns, 360 cartridges, and 500 lbs. of pewter shot." In his formal request for additional cannons, the royal governor requested "a suitable store of shot and powder . . . [to] make Carolina impregnable." In 1703 the Crown approved and funded a building to store additional armament, which was completed in 1713 on what is now Cumberland Street.

The building served its originally intended purpose for many decades, but eventually, it was deemed unnecessary (or too small) and sold into private hands. This multi-gabled, tile-roofed, architectural oddity was almost forgotten by historians until the

Powder Magazine, Charleston
Wikimedia

early 1900s. In 1901 it was purchased by The National Society of The Colonial Dames of America in The State of South Carolina (NSCDA-SC). It was maintained and operated as a small museum until 1991, when water damage, roof deterioration, and time had finally taken too high a toll. The Powder Magazine underwent a $400,000 preservation effort, its first ever. Much-needed archaeological and archival research was also done on the site. The Powder Magazine was reopened in 1997 by the NSC-DA-SC. Inside, an interactive exhibit interprets Charleston's first 50 years—a time when it was still a relatively crude colonial outpost of the British Empire.

Robert Barnwell Rhett House
6 Thomas St., Charleston; privately owned

The fiery discussions that must have taken place here! Most notable as the home of "Fire-eater" Robert Barnwell Rhett (1800–1876), 6 Thomas Street is a landmark house significant to the beginnings of the Civil War. Rhett, who changed his surname from Smith to honor his ancestor, Colonel William Rhett, a leading colonial figure in Charleston, was born in Beaufort, studied law, and began a political career as a state legislator in 1827. He gained a reputation as a states' rights advocate with his staunch opposition to the Tariff of 1828, known in the South as "the Tariff of

Robert Barnwell Rhett House, Charleston
Tina E. Mayland

Robert Barnwell Rhett House, Charleston
Tina E. Mayland

Abominations." Originally nullified, a compromise was later reached reducing the tariffs, but also laid the groundwork for the rise of southern nationalism. In 1837 Rhett was elected to the US House of Representatives where he initially followed John C. Calhoun's political stances. In 1844 Rhett broke with the more moderate Calhoun when he led the Bluffton Movement, which sought a guarantee of state's rights, lower tariffs, and the institution of slavery. Calhoun's opposition, a compromise tariff in 1846, and the annexation of Texas as a slaveholding state doomed the movement, but its ideology would reappear later, and Rhett emerged as the leader of the "fire-eaters" or secessionists in South Carolina.

Rhett denounced the Compromise of 1850 and again called for his home state and the other southern states to leave the Union if their grievances were not met. He served in the US Senate for two years before resigning in 1852 realizing that his views were still considered too radical for most southerners. For the next seven years, he removed himself from politics, but with his son Robert Barnwell Rhett Jr., he acquired the *Charleston Mercury*. The newspaper espoused secession ideals and may have influenced Charleston's leading role in the split from the Union. On the 4th of July in 1859 Rhett gave his first public speech after his seven-year absence calling for South Carolina to secede if a Republican was elected president. At long last on December 20, 1860, South Carolina seceded, and Robert Barnwell Rhett earned his title in history as "Father of Secession."

Rhett and his family lived in the Robert Barnwell Rhett house in Charleston from 1856 to 1863. James Legare built the house in 1833, and it is also known as the Legare-Rhett House. The plan of the house is a Greek Revival wooden frame structure with three-story piazzas (porches). An unusual feature is the large double octagonal rooms on each floor. The Rhett family sold the property to George A. Trenholm, a wealthy businessman and shipowner who successfully breached the Union line with his blockade runners during the Civil War. He was a secretary of the treasury for the Confederacy and is believed to be the "real life" man upon whom Margaret Mitchell based her character Rhett Butler, in her novel *Gone With the Wind*. Another romantic tale connected with the house and its decorative iron gates is one that tells of a young woman who bid farewell to her fiancé as he left for duty in the War Between the States; she promised that she would not reopen the gates until his return. The man was killed in the war, and no owner has opened them since.

Robert William Roper House
9 East Battery, Charleston; classicalamericanhomes.org; admission charged

This stunning residence built in 1838 leaves most visitors awestruck, not just for the monumental scale of the classical Greek Revival architecture, but also its site on Charleston's High Battery overlooking Charleston Harbor and beyond. When Robert William Roper purchased the lot from the City of Charleston, the city had recently built a new sea wall around the southeastern tip of the peninsula, and nothing stood between the site and the harbor. Roper, a state legislator and civic leader, "wanted his house to be the first and most prominent to be seen as visitors

Robert William Roper House, Charleston
Tina E. Mayland

approached Charleston by sea." And how impressive it must have been and still is today. The regal three-story brick structure fronts East Battery on its gable end, and the south-facing piazza with its massive, white Ionic-capped columns command attention along this iconic row of "town" homes built to impress.

Roper's wealth stemmed from the family's cotton plantation and enslaved labor force at Point Comfort, about 15 miles up the Cooper River from the house. The architect is unknown but is believed to have been Charles Friederich Reichardt, a Prussian who studied under Karl Friedrich Schinkel, Germany's famous classical architect. Reichardt was the architect of the Charleston Hotel and both it and Roper

Robert William Roper House, Charleston
Tina E. Mayland

House resemble Schinkel's highly praised Altes Museum in Berlin with a flat roofline in part supported by a long Ionic colonnade elevated above a ground-level arcade.

During the Civil War, the homes along East Battery received extensive shelling by Union troops. One contemporary account noted that "the architectural projection of the porch was blown away by a shell." Additional damage was incurred when Confederate troops were destroying their heavy artillery in advance of General Sherman's army entering South Carolina in February 1865, lest it fall into the enemy's hands. Reportedly, the blasting of the Blakely cannon sent a six-foot-long piece weighing 2,000 pounds into the air landing on Roper House. It settled in the attic and remains there today.

Some of the outstanding interior features include the 3-story circular staircase that sweeps upward past niches with three large classical statues of Greek goddesses of the arts. The double parlors boast 18-foot-tall ceilings, and original black marble mantels and crystal chandeliers with floor-to-ceiling windows looking out to sea. The nearly 200-year-old house has only had a handful of owners who cared for it and largely kept it true to its original design. One exception was Rudolph Siegling, son of music publisher Johann Siegling, and publisher of Charleston's local newspaper, who expanded the house by adding a 60-foot-long ballroom wing and kitchen in the rear while keeping it in the same architectural style. Another owner of note was Richard Hampton Jenrette who purchased it in 1968 for $100,000, a record-setting price in Charleston at the time. Although little of the original furnishings are there, he installed exquisite period appropriate silk-upholstered furniture, custom-made carpets and draperies, and many rare decorative objects. Jenrette considered it "the quintessential antebellum mansion that my *Gone With the Wind*–influenced generation dreamed about owning."

The Roper House was placed in The Classical American Homes Preservation Trust established by Jenrette to protect and preserve his collection of architecturally significant American homes for future generations. (Another of his properties covered in this book is Millford Plantation in the Fall Line chapter.) Roper House is occasionally opened to the public; visit the Trust website for details.

Nathaniel Russell House
51 Meeting St., Charleston; 843-724-8481; historiccharleston.org; open daily year-round for guided tours; admission charged

Prominent shipping merchant Nathaniel Russell decided to build his great "mansionhouse" on Meeting Street, practically within sight of the busy wharves that produced his wealth. When his house was completed in 1808, Russell was 71 years old, and he had reportedly spent $80,000 on the project—an enormous sum at that time.

Nathaniel Russell House, Charleston
Shutterstock

Like the Joseph Manigault House (see above), Russell's new home was inspired by the work of English architect Robert Adam, whose delicate style was influenced by the airy classical designs only recently uncovered (literally) in the Italian excavations of Pompeii and Herculaneum. Its elaborate plasterwork ornamentation, its free-flying staircase floating up through three complete stories without any visible means of support, and its beautiful proportions prompted the celebrated French aristocrat Henry Deas Lesesne to proclaim it to be "beyond all comparison the finest establishment in Charleston."

Today's visitor is also immediately dazzled by the dramatic, elliptical stairway and the bold original colors used throughout, carefully researched by Historic Charleston Foundation. These finely proportioned, geometric rooms are furnished with another outstanding collection of Charleston, English, and French pieces, including rare china, silver, and paintings. Spacious gardens surround this old house adding to its grand feel as another showcase home and a Charleston favorite. Unlike most other Charleston house museums, the Nathaniel Russell House has never been through a sad period of decline and disrepair. First as a fine town house, then as the home of a South Carolina governor, and later as a school for girls, and even a convent, 51 Meeting St. has always been a respected and cared-for landmark. Today it is owned and operated as a house museum by Historic Charleston Foundation, whose ongoing research is revealing more about the craftspeople who built it, and the 18 enslaved men and women who lived in the rear kitchen house working to

Nathaniel Russell House, Charleston
Tina E. Mayland

maintain the Russell home, household, and garden. It was designated a National Historic Landmark in 1973 and is recognized as one of America's finest examples of neoclassical architecture. A combination ticket for this and the Aiken-Rhett house at 48 Elizabeth St. is available.

Edward Rutledge House
The Governor's House Inn
117 Broad St., Charleston; 843-720-2070, 800-720-9812; www .governorshouse.com; limited access

Built in 1760 by James Laurens, brother of Henry Laurens (President of the Second Continental Congress), the house takes its primary name from Edward Rutledge (1749–1800), perhaps the most well-known resident of the home. Rutledge lived in the home, located across the street from his older brother John Rutledge (see below), initially renting it from the Laurens family then purchasing it in1788. A native South Carolinian, he studied law in England just as his brother did and set up a Charleston law practice. He married Henrietta Middleton, daughter of the wealthy rice planter, Henry Middleton (see Middleton Place above). He was elected a delegate to the First and Second Continental Congresses. Soon thereafter Edward Rutledge at just 26 years old became the youngest signer of the Declaration of Independence. As a Revolutionary War soldier, he served as a captain of artillery for the South Carolina militia. Rutledge was captured during the siege of Charleston by the British in 1780

Edward Rutledge House, Charleston
Tina E. Mayland

Edward Rutledge House, Charleston
Tina E. Mayland

and spent time as a prisoner of war in St. Augustine, Florida. He was released in a prisoner exchange and resumed his political career as a representative in the South Carolina House of Representatives (1782-1796) and state senator (1796–98). In ill health he persevered to serve as South Carolina's governor until his death in

Charleston in January 1800. His gravesite is well marked and can be found in St. Philip's churchyard just outside the south entrance to the church.

The large Georgian double house was designed by Miller & Fullerton and conforms to the original symmetry of this architectural style on its exterior. It is a two-story frame house over a high basement with five bays fronting Broad Street and four bays in depth. The hipped roof has a projecting pediment roof covering three bays with a round window over the center of the structure. Greek Revival double piazzas or porches were added later on the east and west sides, although some of the eastern one was removed to add a wing to the home during extensive renovations by Frederick Wagener, owner of a large Charleston grocery company, around 1885. The current exterior was modified into a Colonial Revival style in 1935.

Although much of the interior of the house has been altered due to various uses of the structure over the years, it retains its 18th-century core and many original features such as the heart pine floors, triple-hung 9-foot windows, intricate moldings, and seven fireplaces. But during Wagener's ownership, an elaborate Victorian spiral staircase was installed as well as other interior changes.

This is the oldest house in Charleston currently being used as a bed-and-breakfast. Today, called the Governor's House Inn, the house boasts 11 elegantly appointed guest rooms. Most of the rooms feature original 12-foot ceilings with fireplaces and private verandas. The roofscape room provides lovely views over the peninsula's historic architecture. A stay here is ideal for the location from several standpoints. You're at the edge of the original Grand Modell city of old Charles Towne on the site of the Charleston Orange Garden, an orange grove also used as a park in the late 1600s. It's also within today's prestigious Below Broad residential area, and you're within easy walking distance of King Street's shopping and antiques district.

John Rutledge House
116 Broad St., Charleston; 843-723-7999, 800-476-9741; johnrutledgehouseinn.com; limited access

Built in 1763 by John Rutledge (1739–1800), a governor of South Carolina (1779–82) and a signer of the US Constitution, the house at 116 Broad St. sits on the north side of Broad Street directly across from the home of his younger brother, Edward Rutledge (see above). Both Rutledges played important roles in the American Revolution and founding of the new nation. John Rutledge helped organize the South Carolina patriot forces, served as a member of the First and Second Continental Congresses, attended the 1787 Constitutional Convention, and signed the finalized document. He also served as Senior Associate Justice of the US Supreme Court (1789–91) appointed by President Washington, until he resigned to become Chief

Justice of South Carolina. He was involved in the Stamp Act controversy during his early career establishing himself as one of the foremost legal minds in the country. Washington himself had breakfast here and was one of many patriots, statesmen, and presidents who came to call on Mr. Rutledge. Rutledge lived in the house until his death in 1800 and is buried in St. Michael's churchyard nearby.

John Rutledge House, Charleston
Tina E. Mayland

The house was originally a two-story structure built on top of a raised basement. A third story was added in 1853 by later owner Thomas M. Gadsden. The slate hip roof has a front-facing gable, and the stuccoed exterior has corner quoining with pediments embellishing all the windows. The grey and white tilework on the front sidewalk leads to a double marble staircase curving to the front door. Attributed to blacksmith Christopher Werner, the ornate cast- and wrought-iron railings and second story balcony incorporate palmetto and eagle motifs, enhancing the impressive façade. Visitors to Charleston who have tasted the local delicacy, she-crab soup, will be interested to know that it is believed to

John Rutledge House, Charleston
Tina E. Mayland

have been first served here. A 20th-century owner, Mayor Robert Goodwyn Rhett, employed a butler, William Deas, who is credited with creating and serving it during a visit from President William Howard Taft in 1909.

The John Rutledge House was completely renovated in 1989 and transformed (as part of a three-building complex) into a swank inn with 19 rooms in all. Of these, 8 rooms are in the carriage houses located behind the main house. The property was designated a National Historic Landmark (1973), and the National Trust for Historic Preservation named it among the top 32 Historic Hotels of America. The main residence contains elaborate parquet floors, Italian marble mantels, and molded plaster ceilings. The John Rutledge House Inn rooms have been modernized to include private baths, refrigerators, televisions, and individual climate controls. Afternoon tea is served in the ballroom (open to the public), and evening turndown service includes chocolates at bedside. This inn is part of the Charming Inns of Charleston group and offers a rare opportunity for an overnight visit in a Landmark home.

St. Michael's Church
80 Meeting St., Charleston; (843) 723-0623; stmichaelschurch.net; open Sun through Fri; free

While St. Philip's can claim to be the oldest congregation in Charleston, St. Michael's lays claim to having the oldest church structure (1752–1761). There is some mystery as to whom the actual architect of St. Michael's might have been, but there's no question that this magnificent edifice is one of the great treasures of the city. The church has remained essentially unchanged over the centuries, with the exception of a sacristy added in 1883. However, the structure has undergone major repairs several times because of natural and man-made disasters. In the earthquake of 1886, the steeple tower sank 8 inches, and the church cracked in several places. St. Michael's was damaged by a tornado in 1935 and again in 1989 by Hurricane Hugo. During both the American Revolution and the Civil War, the spire was painted black to make it less visible as a target for enemy gunners.

During his visit to Charleston in 1791, President George Washington worshiped at St. Michael's, where he sat in the Governor's Pew—so marked by a small plaque. In later years, the Marquis de Lafayette and General Robert E. Lee sat in that same pew. Buried in St. Michael's churchyard are several distinguished members of the congregation, including General Charles Cotesworth Pinckney, Revolutionary hero,

St. Michael's Church, Charleston
Shutterstock

St. Michael's Church Steeple, Charleston
Lee Davis Perry

signer of the Constitution, and Federalist presidential candidate; and John Rutledge (see above), signer of the Constitution and member of the US Supreme Court.

Among the most arresting sights and sounds of Charleston are the bells of St. Michael's, which have a fascinating history all their own. They ring every quarter hour in a melodic cascade of tones that sound the same today as when they were first installed in 1764. The eight bronze bells made their first of several long journeys to Charleston across the Atlantic from Whitechapel Foundry of London, England, where they were cast earlier that same year.

Prior to the Revolutionary War, the bells were rung in defiance of the Crown, voicing the city's strong protest against the Stamp Act of 1765. Later, the bells were confiscated by the British and sent back to England as a trophy of war. Once brought to England, the bells ricocheted back to Charleston in 1782 via the generosity of a private investor.

Along came the Civil War and once again the bells were considered at risk, and seven of the eight original bells were sent to Columbia for safekeeping. But General Sherman chose Columbia as an artillery target, and the capital of South Carolina was extensively burned in February of 1865. Only one tenor bell was left in Charleston in St. Michael's steeple to warn the city of encroaching danger. In 1865, the year the city fell, the bell rang dutifully until it cracked. The following year, the vestry sent the charred bells along with the cracked tenor bell back to the Whitechapel Foundry to be recast in the original molds, which miraculously still existed. The bells of St. Michael's had crossed the Atlantic again to be home (seemingly) at long last.

In 1989, however, when Hurricane Hugo hit Charleston, once more the bells were returned to Whitechapel for yet another recasting. This time the work was part of a $3.8 million restoration and repair of St. Michael's undertaken after the storm. And yes, once again, the original molds were used. The bells returned refreshed and renewed on July 4, 1993, and rang out in a day-long concert of traditional hand ringing done in the English style. Visitors are welcome to join Sunday services and visit the church at other times by consulting the website.

St. Philip's Church
146 Church St., Charleston; 843-722-7734; stphilipschurchsc.org; open for services and Tues through Fri tours; free

St. Philip's Church (c. 1835–1838) is the mother church of the Anglican congregations in South Carolina, and for more than 300 years, this church has been a vital force in the life of Charleston. Today, there are more than 1,500 communicants. It is believed the name is derived from the Anglican parish in Barbados, the island from which many early Charleston planters came after immigration from England. The first St. Philip's was built in 1680–1681 on the site of what is now St. Michael's Church at Meeting and Broad Streets. A new edifice was authorized for what was considered to be the "new" gates of the city (the present site on Church Street) in 1710, and the design was influenced by English Baroque church style of the time. Some distinctive features are the triple Tuscan portico reaching out into Church Street reminding passersby to attend church and contemplate spiritual matters.

St. Philip's Church
Tina E. Mayland

Inside fluted Corinthian pillars support a lofty double arcade rising to a vaulted ceiling. The keystones of the arches are adorned with relief sculptures of cherubim reminding parishioners of celestial rewards above. In 1777 Edmund Burke described the church as "spacious, and executed in a very handsome taste, exceeding everything of that kind which we have in America." This building was destroyed by fire in 1835

St. Philip's Church
Joe Perry

but quickly rebuilt retaining many of the previous structure's architectural features. The present building was designed by Joseph Hyde, who was influenced by the neoclassical arches inside London's St. Martin's-in-the-Fields Church (1721) designed by James Gibbs. The graceful, towering steeple (1848–50) is attributed to Charleston architect Edward Brickell White.

Noted 18th-century evangelist, John Wesley, visited and preached at St. Philip's several times. The Reverend Dr. Robert Smith was the rector during the Revolutionary period and also served as the first President of the College of Charleston and the first Bishop of South Carolina. As part of its efforts to spread the Gospel, St. Philip's established one of the earliest schools in the colony and its first hospital. More of the history of Charleston is traceable just by reading the names of the memorial plaques around the walls of the sanctuary and in the churchyard outside. Buried here are Colonel William Rhett, officer of the Crown; Edward Rutledge, signer of the Declaration of Independence; Charles Pinckney, signer of the US Constitution; and the Hon. John C. Calhoun, statesman and vice president of the United States. Here, too, is the grave of Edwin DuBose Heyward, author of *Porgy* and collaborator with George Gershwin for the folk opera *Porgy and Bess*. In addition to services visitors are welcome limited hours on Tuesday through Friday.

Simmons-Edwards House
14 Legare St., Charleston; privately owned

Locally known as the "Pineapple Gate House" the "pineapples" may have been carved originally to depict Italian pinecones. With pineapples symbolizing hospitality it is hard to dissuade gracious Charlestonians otherwise. George Edwards, who

Simmons-Edwards House
Tina E. Mayland

Simmons-Edwards House, Charleston
Tina E. Mayland

purchased the house in 1816, installed the large brick gates with their prominent finials and possibly commissioned an Italian mason in Philadelphia to create them. Other striking features of the gates are the graceful wooden and wrought-iron panels, and, upon close examination, the English tuckpointing of the brickwork. To even out the irregularly shaped red bricks, red-tinted mortar was used to straighten out the lines; a recess in the tinted mortar revealed the white lime mortar joint achieving the precise lines desired. Details count. Proud of his ownership of the property, George Edwards's initials are set within the curved ironwork flanking the marble steps to the refined front entry as well.

The large, distinguished neoclassical single house was built by Francis Simmons, a wealthy Johns Island planter, c. 1800. It was built as his town house perhaps replacing an earlier wooden structure on the site of today's garden. The three-story structure sits on a raised arcaded basement with a two-story side piazza supported by a colonnade of Corinthian columns overlooking the extensively restored formal gardens. The brickwork is laid in a Flemish bond pattern, and the corners of the building have brick quoining lending a solid, stately presence. The windows are six panes over six, double sash. Some of the original outbuildings survive; the two-story kitchen house and the carriage house are joined to the main house by "hyphens" or connecting passageways added in the late 19th century. Separation of the outbuildings from the main house was a fire prevention tactic quite common at the time.

Architecturally significant, the Simmons-Edwards House has a history among Charleston's real estate transactions of selling at the highest price ever paid for a property on several occasions. Among the later notable owners were James Adger Smyth, mayor of Charleston from 1879–1920; Nancy Stevenson, the first female to hold a statewide office as lieutenant governor of South Carolina from 1979–1983; and Andrew Crispo, infamous art dealer, whose court-ordered auction to satisfy his debts, sold the house in 1997 for $3.1 million, again the highest price for a Charleston property at the time.

Snee Farm
1254 Long Point Rd., Mt. Pleasant; 843-881-5516, 843-883-3123; nps.gov/chpi; open daily year-round; free

Snee Farm (Charles Pinckney National Historic Site) was saved from commercial development as recently as 1988. But let's begin with Charles Pinckney, the man. He began his public career at age 22, when he was admitted to the South Carolina Bar and the South Carolina General Assembly. Pinckney served as one of four South Carolina delegates at the Constitutional Convention in Philadelphia.

Often referred to as the "Forgotten Founder," Charles Pinckney presented his "Pinckney Draft" at the Constitutional Convention, which called for a strong central government made up of three "separate and distinct" branches. Some of his adopted contributions to the document included: a legislative branch made up of a Senate and a House of Delegates that would be responsible for "regulating the Trade with the several States as well with Foreign Nations," coining money, and establishing a post office; a judicial branch to settle matters among states and between the federal government and a state; and a president who would be commander in chief and deliver a state of the Union address. He also attached a "Bill of Rights," which provided for "the privilege of the writ of habeas corpus—the trial by jury in all cases,

Snee Farm, Mt. Pleasant
Tina E. Mayland

Snee Farm, Mt. Pleasant
Tina E. Mayland

criminal as well as civil." All in all, more than 25 of his clauses were included in the final draft of the US Constitution, and for this he should no longer be "forgotten."

He later served as governor of South Carolina, was ambassador to Spain from 1801 to 1805, and held seats in both the state and national legislature. He retired from public life in 1821 and died three years later.

Originally, Snee Farm was part of a 500-acre royal grant awarded in 1698 to Richard Butler. By 1754, the farm comprised 715 acres and was purchased that year by Pinckney's father. The property was the family's "country seat" and an integral part of Charles Pinckney's life. Like many other Charleston aristocrats, Pinckney relied on an enslaved labor force (mostly imported from West Africa) to raise the "Carolina gold" (rice) and indigo that was cultivated on Snee Farm. The present house on the remaining 28-acre site, built in the 1820s, is an excellent and charming example of the type of coastal cottage once common here in the Lowcountry. Guests will find interesting interpretive exhibits in and around the house. There's an informative short film telling of Charles Pinckney, Snee Farm, George Washington's colonial era visit to the property, and the United States as a young, emerging nation.

Stono River Slave Rebellion Site
West Bank of Wallace River, Rantowles, Charleston County

Early on the morning of Sunday, September 9, 1739, a group of 20 enslaved Africans led by a literate black man named Jemmy Cato congregated near the Stono River, about 20 miles southwest of Charleston. Their goal: flee south to St. Augustine (some 150 miles away) and attain freedom in Spanish-controlled Florida. Along the way they would garner weapons, attract more enslaved people to join them, and kill anyone who tried to stop them.

Several factors may have contributed to the timing of their revolt—Spanish efforts to instigate insurrection in the shadow of rumored war between England and Spain with escapees rewarded with freedom and land in Florida; a severe yellow fever epidemic in August and September displacing the white population from their plantations and commercial endeavors; and an upcoming provision on September 29 for all white men to carry firearms into their churches on Sunday for added protection.

After gathering at the river, the rebels crossed the Stono Bridge, broke into Hutcheson's store, killing two men, and seizing powder and guns. Next, they burned a house, killed three more people, and reached a tavern all before sunrise. Here, they spared an innkeeper because they deemed him "a good man and kind to his slaves." But other whites were not so lucky; they burned and ransacked 5 houses and killed everyone else they found. Additional enslaved people joined them, and accounts say that from this momentum the insurgents began beating drums, raised a banner, and shouted "Liberty!" to unite their followers and attract more. Around 11 o'clock that morning, Lieutenant Governor William Bull and his party traveling to Charleston came upon the band of rebels, escaping and racing to raise the alarm in Charleston and the surrounding countryside. The insurgents continued southward adding to their ranks now numbering as many as 100 people. One account tells that they then stopped in a field and "set to dancing, Singing and beating drums to draw more Negroes to them."

By late that afternoon the original band had covered about 10 miles. Fatigue and perhaps overconfidence in their numbers, they stopped in an open field near the Jacksonborough ferry to rest before crossing the Edisto River. Here they encountered between twenty and 100 mounted and armed planters and militiamen (perhaps alerted by Bull) and were defeated by the whites in what came to be known as "the battlefield." Regarding many of the rebels as courageous, the victors however acted quickly to suppress the uprising. Some participants were released as they were believed to have been forced to join in, some were shot, and others met an especially gruesome end as they were decapitated with their heads spiked on posts along roadways as a warning to others. Around thirty of the band escaped but were hunted down by the militiamen the following week some thirty miles south; this defeat

Stono River Slave Rebellion Site, Charleston County near Rantowles
Lee Davis Perry

effectively ended the uprising, but a few more rebels were rounded up the following spring, and one leader was captured as late as 1742.

Altogether about forty whites and a comparable number of blacks were killed in the Stono Rebellion (or Cato's Rebellion after leader Jemmy Cato). It was the largest and bloodiest slave revolt in South Carolina and considered the largest uprising in the British mainland colonies to date. Exacerbating fears among the white minority population, more legislation was enacted to maintain control over the majority black population, both enslaved and free. The Negro Act of 1740 stepped up patrol efforts by the militia and required a special act of the legislature for the manumission of enslaved Africans, which previously had been controlled directly by the slaveholder; it restricted gatherings, education, and movement among the blacks; and yet at the same time set up penalties for severe treatment by enslavers, albeit difficult to enforce. It led to a 10-year moratorium on the importation of Africans to curb the growth of the black population in the state. Most of these restrictions remained in effect until the abolishment of slavery after the Civil War.

Colonel John Stuart House
106 Tradd St., Charleston; privately owned

Scottish brogue notwithstanding, Colonel John Stuart must have had a way with words. He had immigrated to North America from Scotland in 1746, eventually settled in Charleston, and was appointed the Superintendent of Indian Affairs for the southern British colonies in 1762. His daunting task was to maintain peaceful relationships with the Native American tribes, specifically the Five Civilized Tribes, inhabiting the region. These tribes were the Cherokee, Chickasaw, Choctaw, Creek (Muscogee), and Seminole.

His first assignment was to inform the tribes of the Proclamation Line of 1763, which was a boundary for containment of English settlers east of the ridge line of the Appalachian Mountains. In December 1763, Stuart met and negotiated with the leaders of the southeastern tribes in Augusta, Georgia. The Treaty of Augusta confirmed the eastern boundary for the Cherokee, pushing them further west than the previous treaty that ended the Cherokee War. It also established a Catawba reservation of 225 square miles on their traditional homeland on the Catawba River; they had requested the reservation for protection from the settlers and other Indian tribes' aggression. Stuart pursued policies addressing unfair

Colonel John Stuart House, Charleston
Tina E. Mayland

Colonel John Stuart House, Charleston
Tina E. Mayland

practices in the very competitive Indian trade seeking a balance between the colonists' and Indians' interests. He controlled the licensing of Indian traders and the transfer of Native American lands. After decades of colonial government control in South Carolina, some were unhappy with Stuart's overriding power. As the Revolutionary War approached, the Charleston Sons of Liberty regarded Stuart as a

Loyalist who was organizing the Indian tribes for war siding with the British. He was arrested in 1775, escaped imprisonment, and fled to West Florida. There, he continued to incite the tribes to oppose the patriots in the southern interior until his death in March 1779.

The finely fitted house he built c. 1772 is considered a rare example of a side-passage plan from colonial times. The front entry on the left side of the front façade opens to a side hall extending all the way to the staircase in the rear of the house. The entry itself is one of the most highly decorated, beautiful door surrounds in the city with its pedimented gable, curved transom window, and matching fluted Corinthian columns. The windows are topped with gabled pediments as well with bracketed lintels underneath. Other exterior features of the three-story structure are the flush mounted wooden siding, hip roof, and a balustraded captain's walk atop. The interior woodwork was so finely executed that the Minneapolis Institute of Arts purchased some of it in the 1920s for a period room display. Thankfully, a later owner, architectural historian John Mead Howells, who purchased the Colonel John Stuart House as a winter home in 1934, had the woodwork reproduced and installed in the house. He also added a second story to the side polygonal wing and piazzas added in the 19th century. He supported other preservation work taking hold in Charleston in the 1930s and 1940s lending his expertise to local advocates rallying to protect Charleston's magnificent collection of 18th- and 19th-century architecture.

Unitarian Church
8 Archdale St., Charleston; 843-723-4617; www.charlestonuu.org; regular Sunday services; free

They say timing is everything and, in fact, the church here got off to rough start. The first building on this site was under construction when the American Revolution began. During the British occupation of the city, the church was chosen as quarters for the British militia, and its newly installed pews were destroyed. Undeterred the church, of Georgian design, was finally repaired and in use by 1787 as the Second Independent Church. For the next 30 years, it formed one corporate body with the Independent Congregational Church at the White Meeting House (now Circular Congregational Church; see earlier Parish House listing).

The first pastor was Rev. Anthony Forster who was a Unitarian minister. Next was Dr. Samuel Gilman who served the congregation from 1819 to 1858. He is also known for his enduring anthem to his alma mater, "Fair Harvard." His wife, Caroline Gilman, published the first children's newspaper in the country called the *Rosebud*. She also designed the gardens on the south side of the church and a Gothic monument to the Gilmans can be seen here. In 1839, this congregation was rechartered as the Unitarian Church, a first in the South.

Unitarian Church, Charleston
Lee Perry Davis

Charleston was experiencing a period of great prosperity in the 1850s, and the Unitarians hired the young architect (and church member) Francis D. Lee to remodel the building in the popular Gothic Revival style. He was commissioned to incorporate the old walls and tower into his new design. Lee was inspired by the Henry VII chapel at Westminster Abbey—especially the delicate and lacy fan

Unitarian Churchyard, Charleston
Lee Perry Davis

tracery ceiling there. He duplicated that amazing ceiling in this church, and it is considered to be some of the finest Gothic Revival work extant in America.

If you visit the church, don't be put off by the graveyard; it always catches visitors off guard. People are struck by what seems to be benign neglect as the grounds appear overgrown in a tangle of briars, vines, weeds, and flowers gone to seed. Nothing could be further from the truth. The congregation jealously guards this horticultural chaos as a time capsule of 19th-century funerary art and botanical tributes to loved ones long gone. Many of these wild plants and flowers are almost forgotten varieties not found in any seed catalog or florist's inventory today. It's even a part of The Garden Club of Charleston's Gateway Walk departing from the usual sidewalk view winding through historic churchyards and gardens for four blocks of the old city. A pleasant stroll that feels like almost like stepping through time.

Yorktown (USS)
40 Patriots Point Rd., Mt. Pleasant; 843-884-2727, 866-831-1720; patriotspoint.org; open daily year-round; parking fee and admission charged

As far as landmarks go . . . no one comes or goes through Charleston via US 17 across the dramatic Arthur Ravenel Jr. Bridge over the Cooper River without noticing the giant aircraft carrier moored off Mt. Pleasant. It dominates—no, commands—a vast stretch of the Cooper's Mt. Pleasant shore at the very gates into Charleston Harbor. She is none other than the USS *Yorktown* (CV-10), the famous "Fighting Lady" of World War II and the proud flagship of Patriots Point Naval & Maritime Museum.

USS **Yorktown**, *Mt. Pleasant*
iStock

Originally named *Bon Homme Richard*, it was renamed in honor of the *Yorktown* (CV-5) after it was sunk at the famous Battle of Midway in June 1942. The new ship was commissioned on April 15, 1943, after a mere 16½ months of construction in Newport News, Virginia. Later that year USS *Yorktown* (CV-10) began service in the Pacific offensive participating in numerous battles until the surrender of Japan in 1945. The famous "Fighting Lady" served in combat at Truk, the Marianas, Iwo Jima, and Okinawa in World War II. Shortly after the ship was commissioned and sent into battle, 20th Century Fox put a film crew onboard to record—on then-rare Technicolor film—the continuing war story of a typical Navy carrier in action. The spectacular footage shot at unnamed, secret locations during then-unnamed battles became the Academy Award–winning documentary film feature of 1944. The film was called *The Fighting Lady*, and it is shown daily at the *Yorktown's* onboard theater at regularly scheduled intervals. Don't miss it. Nothing brings the World War II drama of the *Yorktown* to life like this amazing celluloid time capsule. The terrible explosions and blistering fires, the fierce fighting, and all the brave young faces who served on the *Yorktown* are there to be seen and appreciated by generations then unborn.

After the war, it was updated as an attack carrier for jet aircraft and then re-designated as an anti-submarine aircraft carrier in 1957. In addition to its 11 battle stars earned for WWII service, 5 more were added for service off Vietnam from 1965 to 1968. Next the ship picked up the crew of Apollo VIII, the first manned

USS Yorktown *at Patriots Point, Mt. Pleasant*
Wikimedia

spacecraft to circle the moon. The *Yorktown* was decommissioned in 1970 and relocated to Charleston to become the centerpiece of the new Patriot's Point Naval & Maritime Museum.

The hangar and flight decks of the carrier are now set up as a journey through the history of naval aviation. Here you'll see many of the prop-driven fighters, bombers, and torpedo planes that fought throughout the Pacific. You'll see a B-25 bomber similar to the ones of General Jimmy Doolittle's famous "Sixty Seconds Over Tokyo" raid in addition to fighters that provided the air support during the Korean War. A great collection of some of the world's most feared jets is displayed here, along with distinguished battle histories spanning from Korea to Desert Storm. You'll see the actual living quarters of the pilots and the "ready rooms" where they were briefed on their upcoming missions.

You will also find the destroyer USS *Laffey* (see above), which can be boarded, inspected, and photographed at your leisure. Another exhibit in the complex is the Vietnam War Naval Support Base, showing the living conditions and work areas of a typical support base. The Cold War Submarine Memorial features a full-sized replica of a Fleet Ballistic Missile submarine with educational stations that pay tribute to those who served our country in naval submarines from 1947 to 1989. You'll also find the newly renovated and expanded Medal of Honor Museum, featuring interactive displays representing the different eras of military history in which the Medal of Honor was awarded. You'll see actual Medals of Honor and some of the artifacts related to their original recipients. For this complex, one of Charleston's major attractions, you'll need comfortable shoes and plenty of time.

Chapter 2
THE SOUTHERN CORNER

Beaufort Historic District
**Visitor Center, 713 Craven St.; Beaufort; 843-525-8500; beaufortsc
.org; Mon through Sat, 10 a.m. to 4 p.m.**

Beaufort, the second oldest town in the state, was formally chartered by the English
in 1711. It was sited on Port Royal Island, one of 65 islands contained in present-day
Beaufort County in the heart of the Lowcountry, midway between Charleston and
Savannah, GA. It grew into an important shipbuilding center, and indigo, rice, and
later sea island cotton-producing area, but frequent hostilities from the native Indian
tribes and foreign invaders checked its early growth. The British constructed Fort
Frederick in 1735 to protect its interests here.

A mere seven months after the outbreak of the Civil War, victory at the Battle
of Port Royal Sound gave the Union strategic control of the area south of Charleston around Beaufort. During the war the town was occupied by Union forces,
which saved it from being burned and
destroyed. As the planters and city residents fled, most of their slaves were left
behind. Thus, it became one of the first
places in the country to carve out a place
for the newly freed slaves both during
the war and the period afterward,
known as Reconstruction.

Today the big homes looking out
over the inlet and the ocean are almost
exactly as they were in 1860. You can
get a very good idea of the look of the
old town and its surroundings from any
one of the following movies filmed here:
*Glory, The Big Chill, The Great Santini,
Forrest Gump, Conrack,* and *The Prince
of Tides.* As a matter of fact, Pat Conroy,
author of many of these titles, spent his

Beaufort Historic District
Lee Davis Perry

Beaufort Historic District Visitors Center
Lee Davis Perry

childhood here and later taught school a little way down the coast out on Daufuskie Island. And as another matter of fact, the cast of *The Prince of Tides*—Barbra Streisand, Nick Nolte, and Jeroen Krabbé—all stayed downtown at the Rhett House Inn, one of the old historic mansions that has been converted to bed-and-breakfast inns. Subsequently, the picturesque, charming city has embraced tourism breathing new life into the once sleepy, small town. The military is the largest employer with the Marine Corps Air Station, the Naval Hospital, and the Parris Island Marine Training Depot nearby.

Your first stop should be the Visitor Information Center at 713 Craven St., inside the crenellated walls of the Arsenal (1798). Here you can pick up a walking-tour map with points of particular interest denoted within the 304 acres making up the original town. If you feel up to walking a few miles (approximately within a three-mile radius), just follow the dotted lines leading you to 34 historical sites beginning with the Beaufort Museum, a fascinating repository of the city's man-made history, just steps across from the Visitor Center. Or take a horse-drawn carriage tour at a leisurely, clip-clop pace. And afterward stroll along the pleasant waterfront park for dining, shopping, or just "taking the air." If you do, you will appreciate why the old city was listed on the National Register of Historic Places in 1969 and designated a National Historic Landmark in 1973.

Charlesfort—Santa Elena Site

USMC Parris Island Museum, Bldg. #11, Marine Corps Recruit Depot, Parris Island, Port Royal; (843) 228-2951; parrisislandmuseum.com; daily 10 a.m. to 4:30 p.m. (closed major holidays)

Over 450 years ago French explorer Jean Ribaut sailed into Port Royal Sound, the second deepest natural harbor on the East Coast, near present-day Beaufort. In addition to the French, the Spanish and English all competed to acquire for their respective kings and countries lands in the New World along the southeastern seaboard and beyond. But each struggled to colonize this isolated coastal area amid constant threat from each other as well as the American Indian tribes long established there.

Technically, the Spanish were the first Europeans to enter these waters in 1514, but Ribaut claimed the Port Royal harbor and established a French Huguenot settlement called Charlesfort in 1562. But it was short-lived and abandoned the following year. The Spanish, attempting to lay claim to La Florida (an area spanning present-day Florida, Georgia, and the Carolinas), quickly established a garrison in St. Augustine in 1565 and then set their sights on the abandoned French site. In 1566 the Spanish naval officer Pedro Menéndez de Avilés returned and built Fort San Felipe and the settlement called "Santa Elena" at the same location, now known as Parris Island. Serving as the first colonial capital of Spanish Florida beginning in 1569, Santa Elena endured until 1587 when a combination of factors—among them fire, disease, Indian attacks, and food shortages—diminished the stronghold. Also, the British led by Sir Francis Drake were threatening invasion as Drake worked his way up the coast from the Caribbean raiding other Spanish villages. As a result, King Philip II of Spain decided to consolidate his settlements moving the Santa Elena colonists to St. Augustine.

But it is important to note that this European settlement pre-dates both Jamestown and Plymouth—another South Carolina first! Lots of ongoing archaeological work continues to uncover more details about the day-to-day life of the colonists living first in Charlesfort and then Santa Elena. Site work at Santa Elena reveals more than 40 colonial buildings surrounding a central plaza where 200 or so Catholic missionaries, farmers, and families worked and lived. The site is physically located within the US Marine Corps Recruit Depot at Parris Island in Port Royal, SC, and was designated a National Historic Landmark in 2001. The USMC Parris Island Museum is a repository for many of the artifacts and talks more about the island's history and early inhabitants up to the present day with a focus on the US Marine Corps.

The Santa Elena History Center at 1501 Bay Street in downtown Beaufort is another must-stop and tells "America's Untold Story" in an introductory film.

Charlesfort—Artist's Rendition of Santa Elena
The Parris Island Museum, USMC

A self-paced tour takes visitors through the main exhibit revealing our country's earliest history. Kids will enjoy the Archaeology Learning Exhibit where they can discover (replica) artifacts similar to the ones found by the archaeological teams working at the Santa Elena site. Another teaching exhibit describes the challenges of 16th-century navigation across the Atlantic Ocean. Different Spanish vessels are depicted, as well as the preparations involved for the long journey, and the rigors of shipboard life. It also explains how the Spanish, using nothing more than an astrolabe, compass, and cross staff, were able to navigate successfully in this unfamiliar world. The history of the Santa Elena History Center itself may hold interest for some visitors. The building once served as a prestigious private residence, a hospital during the Civil War, and a county courthouse. The jail cells are a popular photo op. The Center is open Tuesday through Saturday from 10 a.m. to 4 p.m. More information is available at santa-elena.org or (843) 379-1550.

Fig Island
Edisto Island; dnr.sc.gov; no access

The time: roughly 4,400 to 3,500 years ago in the Late Archaic Period.

The place: three shell middens (mounds) in the vast salt marsh surrounding what was later named Edisto Island for the Edistow tribe who greeted the English in the late 1600s along coastal South Carolina.

The people: hunter-gatherers who were piling shells on the site at the same time as the Egyptians were constructing the earliest pyramids.

Exactly what happened on this site (and more than 30 other shell ring sites scattered along the southeastern coast) is somewhat of a mystery, but what is known without doubt is that these early people used or ingested vast quantities of oysters and other shellfish, which were so abundant in surrounding creeks and estuaries that the supply was virtually endless. Over time these discarded shells piled up in a pattern that changed the landscape. Whether or not these shellfish were consumed for daily sustenance or feasting or processed for some other purpose is still not clear. But the shell middens that remain after thousands of years of hurricanes, erosion, rising sea levels, and natural decomposition still stand. The largest shell formation rises steeply up to 6 meters high above mean sea level. It is mysteriously arranged in a ring with a diameter that measures up to 157 meters at its widest point. Additional smaller rings attach to it, as well as a shell mound connected by a shell ramp. Two

Fig Island, Edisto
South Carolina Historic Properties Record

other shell rings make up the site, one forming a half circle and one in a six-sided symmetrical shape topped with rims of animal and fish bones and pottery sherds (fragments) interspersed among the shells. Interior "plazas" are generally clear of all debris. All confirm the sedentary life of the coastal people at the time living in more permanent settlements and purposefully erecting these structures, which indicate use for more than 400 years.

Precisely what role the shells played in the ceremonial life of these early people is unknown, but the sheer volume of this discarded material is certainly provocative and has led to several conflicting theories. Some archaeologists have said these shell formations are what remained from some kind of fish trap; another theory is these shells are remnants of foundations of structures long gone that were dwellings or ceremonial centers for the community. There is some evidence of alignment with the sun and stars. Or perhaps it was some combination of all (or none) of these conjectures evolving over time. For now the enigma continues.

Unfortunately, ongoing archaeological study and fragility of the site prohibit any public access at this time. The large size and complexity of the Fig Island rings as well as its well preserved condition make it one of the most important shell ring sites in our country. Hopefully, in the future carefully placed observation platforms and boardwalks may offer an up close and personal visit with the site for us to better understand some of our earliest North American people and their way of life.

(For those seeking a similar site that is accessible to the public, the See Wee Shell Ring is located north of Charleston in the Francis Marion National Forest off US Highway 17. A mile-long trail and boardwalk with several interpretative stops winds through the site, and more information can be found at www.fs.fed.us.)

Marshlands
501 Pinckney St., Beaufort; privately owned

The James Robert Verdier House, also known as "Marshlands," is a red hipped roof, white wood frame house built from 1810-1814 that proudly and serenely fronts the marsh along the Beaufort River. It is located on a large lot at Pinckney and Federal Streets within the Beaufort Historic District, specifically in "The Old Point" area, so called for its eastern-facing point of land jutting out into the river. Historians deem the structure to be West Indian in its architectural roots resembling a Barbadian plantation house, but Beaufortonians consider it a quintessential Beaufort-style dwelling with a wrap-around porch supported by simple tapered columns. The lower-level arcade foundation is made of tabby painted a pale pink similar to other historic homes of this era. Tabby was a common building material at the time mixing local oyster shells, lime, and water. The arched basement raises the main level one-story above ground, always a good idea when facing potentially rising tidal

Marshlands, Beaufort
Lee Davis Perry

Marshlands, Beaufort
Lee Davis Perry

water. Double, side-facing staircases lead up to the porch landing and the waterfront entrance. In addition to capturing gentle breezes, the porch offers a lovely view of the river across to neighboring Lady's Island.

The eleven-room interior is elegantly outfitted in the Federal style with graceful fanlights over doorways, tripartite windows, and fine moldings. More Federal details include high quality, original Adam-influenced mantelpieces in the dining room and drawing room. Other special features are reeded woodwork and a Palladian window spilling light on the spiral staircase leading to the third level of the house.

Of special note, is that the original owner of the home was Dr. Verdier, a physician who devised a treatment for yellow fever that successfully combated this widespread fatal disease so prevalent in the Lowcountry. Son of merchant and planter John Mark Verdier, Dr. Verdier's house is sometimes confused with his father's home, the Verdier House (c. 1804) on Bay Street, now the main office of Historic Beaufort Foundation. During the Civil War the James Robert Verdier House became the headquarters for the US Sanitary Commission started in 1861 to take care of wounded Union soldiers. The moniker, "Marshlands," is relatively new and had its origins from the name of a fictional Beaufort home in the 1931 novel, *A Sea Island Lady*, by Francis Griswold. Marshlands is not open to the public, but on occasion it is a venue for special events and historic home tours.

Penn Center Historic District
P.O. Box 126, St. Helena Island; (843) 838-2432; penncenter.com; museum admission charged; grounds are free; Mon through Sat, 11 a.m. to 4 p.m.

Crossing the old swing bridge from downtown Beaufort, you'll reach one of the sea islands, St. Helena Island, which is arguably the center of the Gullah culture and language in our country. These inhabitants of the South Carolina coast are the only group of African Americans who have been able to trace their roots to the villages of the Sierra Leone territory in West Africa. This heritage is shown most dramatically in their knowledge of rice agriculture, cast-net fishing, and arts and crafts such as the distinctive coiled basketry or sweetgrass baskets, and these skills continue to be passed down through the generations. They adapted their native language and music, which evolved into a distinctive collection of words, sounds, and rhythms, during their enslaved lives in this region of the American South.

The Penn Center Historic District on St. Helena is an active, still viable icon of Gullah/Geechee culture and African American history. The Penn School named for Pennsylvania's William Penn was one of the first schools established to educate newly freed African Americans. The date was 1862, several months before Lincoln's Emancipation Proclamation on January 1, 1863. The population this remarkable school served consisted of several thousand African Americans who had been abandoned on the Sea Islands when the local plantation owners fled from Union occupation during the Civil War. Two northern missionaries, Laura Towne and Ellen Murray, arrived in 1862 to begin this work, which became known as "The Port Royal Experiment." The two idealistic, highly dedicated women spent the next 40 years of their lives refining their task to meet the needs of these disenfranchised, uneducated people.

By 1900 the mission of what was now called Penn Normal Industrial and Agricultural School had expanded beyond basic literacy. It included carpentry, cobbling, wheel-wrighting, blacksmithing, agricultural sciences, and teacher training to broaden its outreach and effectiveness. Penn-educated teachers spread throughout the Sea Islands taking with them the skills, tools, and enlightenment of education.

Penn School Historic District Reconstruction Era National Park
Lee Davis Perry

The school closed in 1948 but evolved into the Penn Community Services Center, an agency of advocacy for the self-sufficient Sea Islanders and that work continues today through festivals, conferences, and grassroots political initiatives.

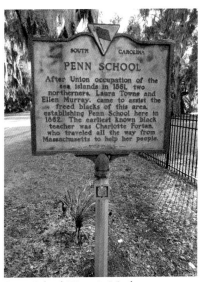

At one point in the 1960s Dr. Martin Luther King Jr. and members of the Southern Christian Leadership Conference (SCLC) used the Center as a retreat and training site for key strategies for the Civil Rights Movement including the famous 1963 March on Washington, DC.

The Penn Center today recalls that remarkable arc through history from slavery through Reconstruction to the social change of the Civil Rights

Penn School Historic Marker
Lee Davis Perry

Movement. The center has 25 buildings, including cottages for groups of up to 100, and a small museum dedicated to the language and culture of the blacks from this region. The 50-acre historic campus is open to visitors and is used for retreats, family reunions, and weddings. The Center sponsors the Annual Penn Center Heritage Days Celebration every November and maintains the York W. Bailey Museum and the Courtney P. Siceloff Welcome Center and Gift Shop. Penn Center is a part of the Gullah Geechee Cultural Heritage Corridor and the Reconstruction Era National Historic Park. It was designated as one of South Carolina's four National Historic Landmark Districts, and the state's only African American one, in 1974.

Robert Smalls House
511 Prince St., Beaufort; privately owned

Also known as the McKee-Smalls House, this home is located at the corner of Prince and New Streets in "The Old Point" area of historic Beaufort. Built by John McKee in 1843, the house is a large wood frame structure with a side gable roof and a south-facing, two-story portico on the front façade. The Federal detailing inside is similar to that in houses built in Beaufort from decades earlier. The parlor over-mantel wood-work is especially reminiscent of decorative woodwork displaying corner sunbursts framing an ellipse found in the John Mark Verdier house dating from 1805 on Bay Street. But the house is best known for another reason—one of its later owners.

Robert Smalls House, Beaufort
Lee Davis Perry

Robert Smalls was born into slavery in 1839 in a cabin behind the house and served in the McKee household until 1851. At the age of twelve he was sent to Charleston where he was "hired out" as a laborer, waiter, and sailor earning wages for his enslaver. Leading up to the Civil War, Smalls found work as a stevedore loading Sea Island cotton, a major export, onto northern ships. Later he became an expert rigger, absorbing waterfront knowledge studying charts, channels, currents, and tides, and noting the locations of shoals and reefs in Charleston Harbor. By July 1861, the Confederates hired him as a deck hand on the former cotton steamer turned transport vessel, *Planter*. They soon recognized his seamanship capabilities and promoted him to wheelsman by March 1862.

The ship transported troops and supplies to fortifications around the city as Smalls successfully navigated it in and out of harbor inlets. As a trusted civilian pilot, he learned all the secret Confederate codes and signals for passing the harbor forts. Seizing just the right moment, he plotted to commandeer the ship filled with Rebel guns and ammunition and turn it over to the Union forces blockading Charleston. On May 13, 1862, with himself, his family, and crew at great risk, he successfully maneuvered past the lookouts. He delivered the ship to the commander of the Union ship, *Onward*, which was preparing to fire on *Planter* until Smalls raised a white flag of surrender. He was catapulted to national fame at the age of 23 when the northern newspapers pronounced him the "First Hero of the Civil War."

Smalls was promptly retained as permanent pilot of the now Union vessel, and he proved to be extremely valuable for his experience and knowledge of Confederate troop locations, fortifications, and waterway mine placements. His fame later led to

Robert Smalls House, Beaufort
Lee Davis Perry

speaking engagements and political exposure in northern cities, and he was awarded the sum of $1,500 prize money by Congress for his role in abducting the *Planter*.

After the war ended, he returned to Beaufort with his family and used his prize money to purchase at government auction the McKee House, in which he and his mother had been enslaved. For the rest of his life, he held several local and state political offices supporting public education for all, construction of public roads, improved train service, and the regulation of pilots in South Carolina ports. In 1875 his political life culminated in election to the Forty-fourth Congress, representing the 5th Congressional District. "The Gullah Statesman" went on to serve for five terms in Congress championing human rights and equal opportunity for all citizens. Today, Robert Smalls Parkway runs through Beaufort, and the Robert Smalls House was made a National Historic Landmark in 1973.

Chapter 3
THE GRAND STRAND

Atalaya and Brookgreen Gardens
1931 Brookgreen Dr., Murrells Inlet; 843-235-6000; brookgreen .org; open daily, 9:30 a.m. to 5 p.m.; admission charged (good for seven consecutive days)

Seeking a warmer climate for his beloved wife's ailing health, industrialist/philanthropist Archer Huntington and sculptor Anna Hyatt Huntington traveled south along the Intracoastal Waterway from New York on their yacht in 1929. The couple became enthralled with the Carolina Lowcountry and soon purchased four adjacent 18th- and 19th-century plantations: The Oaks, Springfield, Laurel Hill, and (old) Brookgreen in the Waccamaw River area. They began designing a winter home and garden at the same time on the combined nine thousand acres. Construction of their home began in 1931 and continued for three years intermittently between work on

Atalaya, Murrells Inlet
Joe Perry

the garden. Mr. Huntington insisted that local labor be employed for the construction, wishing to create work for area residents struggling during the Great Depression. They called the home, "Atalaya," Spanish for watchtower. Archer Huntington was a noted scholar of Spanish history and indulged his passion by designing the house in the Moorish style of architecture found along the Mediterranean coast.

The one-story building was laid out in a square shape with a central, open courtyard. The front wall faced the beach and the Atlantic Ocean, and it contained, along with its two adjoining perimeter walls, 30 rooms that made up the living areas. These consisted of several bedrooms and baths, a dining room, kitchen, sunroom, library, and servants' quarters. Mr. Huntington's study, his secretary's office, and Mrs. Huntington's indoor and outdoor studios made up the southern wing. Since Anna Huntington often sculpted animals in her work, horse stables, dog kennels, and even a bear pen were part of the facilities. At Atalaya the 40-foot tall, central "watchtower" served a very utilitarian purpose other than its architectural legacy. It contained a 3,000-gallon, cypress-lined water tank that created the necessary water pressure for running water throughout the house. The Huntington's new winter residence paid homage to South Carolina with the landscaping of the inner courtyard. There Archer Huntington specified the abundant planting of the sabal (or common name "cabbage") palmetto, the state tree of South Carolina. Today, the unfurnished house and its 3½-mile oceanfront site make up Huntington Beach State Park on US Highway 17 South.

Directly across the highway from Atalaya, the garden they set out to create at Brookgreen Plantation was to be unlike any other. Archer Huntington envisioned the space as a tribute to his wife's art and a testament of his love for her. Anna took her inspiration from him and sketched out the design of the garden walkways in the shape of a butterfly with outstretched wings. She incorporated into the central space the original homesite and magnificent allée of oaks from its early plantation days. Six large millstones that had been used for hulling rice were placed about a terrace. A serpentine, open brickwork wall was built to define the grounds without closing in the spectacular landscape. Mr. Huntington saw that plaques engraved with the verses of great poets adorned niches in the walls, complementing the inspirational and meditative quality of the garden's experience. They quickly realized that the treasure they had discovered for themselves was beginning to take on a larger life. In 1931, they set up a private, non-profit organization with the goal of showcasing American figurative sculpture set within an outdoor surrounding of native plants and animals. Anna Huntington invited other sculptors to place their work there, and it soon became renowned as the place to view some of the best sculpture of the 19th and 20th century. The following year the gardens were opened to the public, and Brookgreen became the first sculpture garden in the United States. Beginning with the stunning, monolithic "Fighting Stallions" by Anna Hyatt Huntington at

Atalaya and Brookgreen Gardens, Murrells Inlet
Joe Perry

the Gardens' entrance, Brookgreen contains more than 2,000 works of American sculpture by 430 artists, among them Lena Goodacre, Gertrude Vanderbilt Whitney, Augustus Saint-Gaudens, Paul Manship, Gutzon Borglum, and Daniel Chester French, and the collection is still growing. It is now acclaimed as the world's finest collection of American figurative sculpture. And today the property is managed by a private organization, Brookgreen Gardens, a Society for the Southeastern Flora and Fauna. In addition to the sculpture garden, Lowcountry history tours and Gullah Geechee programs exploring the African American experience are popular options to explore.

Hampton Plantation
1950 Rutledge Rd., McClellanville; 843-546-9361; southcarolinaparks.com/Hampton; grounds open year-round at no charge; mansion guided tours only Fri through Tues, admission charged

Set back from US Highway 17 about 2 miles, near McClellanville, this is one of the finest examples of antebellum architecture in the entire South. Built in the colonial era, it became a lucrative plantation in the Santee Delta region for the Rutledge,

Hampton Plantation, McClellanville
Lee Davis Perry

Horry, and Pinckney families. Acknowledging the prominence of the families there, many of whom had played a significant role in the founding of the nation, the new president of the United States, George Washington paid a call for breakfast on his trip to the South in 1791. In anticipation of his visit the plantation house was spiffed up with a new coat of paint, and a handsome front portico with eight big columns was built expressly for the occasion. It was finished just in the nick of time. As the story goes…after breakfast the hosts and the presidential party were standing on the portico when the subject came up about a young live oak sprout in front of the house. The question was: Should the tree stay and be allowed to grow up or should it go? Washington had an opinion, which was let the oak grow. The "Washington Oak" still stands today.

When Henry Middleton Rutledge departed Hampton to serve the Confederacy during the Civil War, he left behind one of the grandest homes and most prosperous agricultural enterprises in America. The decades before the Civil War witnessed the high point of rice cultivation in South Carolina, and Hampton Plantation was one of the leaders. At this time Hampton was using the daily action of the tides on the freshwater rivers to irrigate the fields, skillfully tended by enslaved African Americans.

When Colonel Rutledge returned to Hampton Plantation in 1865, he returned to an entirely different South, one in which Hampton Plantation would never again hold the position it once had as a center of political and economic life in the state. The grand house remained unpainted and in decay; cotton was stored in the grand ballroom; crops were planted among the live oaks on the once stately lawn. By 1923 both the colonel and his wife were dead, and the house stood abandoned.

The colonel's son, Archibald Hamilton Rutledge—outdoorsman, writer, and the first poet laureate of South Carolina—returned to Hampton from teaching school in Pennsylvania and at age 56 began a long process of renovating the mansion. He described his labor of love in his best-known book, *Home by the River*: "When I first came back, it was sagging in places and it had not been painted in a generation. Now everything has been done to restore it without changing it and it gleams under its four coats of white paint. It is no unusual thing for visitors to tell me that in its simple dignity it is the most impressive home they have ever seen."

Now protected under the auspices of Hampton Plantation State Park, it serves as an interpretive site to demonstrate how the system of slavery helped build South Carolina coastal plantations into large wealth producers in the early days of the country. An additional website, south-carolina-plantations.com/charleston/hampton .html, traces the lineage of the families and the fascinating history that took place here. (While you are in the vicinity, stop by St. James-Santee Episcopal Church; see below.)

Hopsewee
494 Hopsewee Rd., Georgetown; 843-546-7891; hopsewee.com; open Tues through Sat for guided tours; admission charged

"We were all pleased with Mr. Lynch . . . He is a solid, firm, judicious man" wrote John Adams in 1774 while Thomas Lynch Sr., was attending the First Continental Congress in Philadelphia. Another patriot, Silas Deane of Connecticut, added more about Lynch's character and stature, "[He] is plain, sensible, above ceremony, and carries with more force in his very appearance than most powdered folks in their conversation. He wears his hair straight, his clothes in the plainest order, and is highly esteemed."

Thomas Lynch was born in St. James-Santee Episcopal Parish, the son of a wealthy rice planter who owned several plantations and numerous enslaved workers along the Santee River. Around 1740 he built a new home for his family, sited on a high bluff of the North Santee, called Hopsewee Plantation. He had three children with his wife, Elizabeth Allston. Their only son, Thomas Lynch Jr., was born in 1749 and raised at Hopsewee. He was given a privileged education, first attending the Indigo Society School in Georgetown, some 13 miles away, then to England to attend Eton, Cambridge, and to study law at the Middle Temple, London.

Thomas Lynch Jr. returned home in 1772 and instead of pursuing a law career became a planter at another family plantation, Peach Tree, nearby. But just like his father, he soon became swept up in the tidal wave of seeking independence from Britain. He was elected to the First and Second Provincial Congresses of South Carolina (1774–1776) and was on the constitutional committee for the state. When his father suffered a stroke while attending the Second Continental Congress in

Hopsewee, Georgetown
Wikimedia

Philadelphia in 1776, South Carolina sent him as a delegate to assist his now par-alyzed father. He was only 26 years old, making him the second youngest attendee; his father was still a delegate but too ill to sign the Declaration of Independence. Per-haps it was some solace that his son, Thomas Lynch Jr., was among the signers. As the two men journeyed back home, Thomas Lynch Sr. suffered a second stroke and died in Annapolis, Maryland. Thomas Jr. was also in poor health from a fever he had contracted earlier while serving as a captain in the First South Carolina Regiment during the Revolutionary War. He returned to his plantation to recover but kept his hand in public life as a representative for St. James-Santee Episcopal Parish at the General Assembly (1776–1778). In December 1779 he and his wife, Elizabeth Shubrick, set sail for southern France in the hopes of improving his health; their ship was lost at sea.

Hopsewee was sold in 1762 to Robert Hume for the sum of £5,000. When it was built by Thomas Lynch Sr., the two-story home was constructed with black cypress wood elevated on a stuccoed brick foundation topped by a hip roof. It has a symmetrical layout of four rooms on each floor with double brick chimneys. It might be said that it reflects the "solid, firm, judicious" nature of its builder. As it was passed down in the Hume/Lucas family, it was maintained, renovated, and a double piazza (porch) was added across the front (waterside) to capture welcome prevailing breezes from the Santee delta. As one story goes . . . John Hume, who had inherited Hopsewee after the Revolution, even turned down a Scottish earldom in favor of remaining the "Earl of Marshmud" at his home in South Carolina. The family kept the property for nearly 200 years before it was sold and opened to the public serving as a house museum and event venue today.

Joseph H. Rainey House
909 Prince St., Georgetown; privately owned

Among many of South Carolina's "firsts" is one that may not be familiar to most. Joseph Hayne Rainey, born and raised in Georgetown, was the first black man to serve in the US House of Representatives. He was born into slavery as the child of enslaved parents Edward and Grace Rainey in 1832. His father was hired out as a barber, giving a portion of his earnings back to his enslaver as required by law, but saving until he was finally able to purchase his family's freedom. They moved to Charleston in 1846 where he became a barber at the elite Mills House Hotel and purchased two enslaved people himself. Joseph received a limited education due to the restrictive laws of the time but was trained in the barber trade by his father.

In 1859 Joseph Rainey married his wife, Susan, and worked as a barber until the Civil War broke out. In 1861 his life dramatically changed as did the lives of so many others. The Confederate Army pressed him into service, first digging trenches for fortifications around Charleston, then working as a cook and a steward on a blockade runner slipping supplies through the Union's naval blockade. Rainey and his wife escaped to Bermuda where they found a more favorable environment; slavery had been abolished in 1834, and the economy was booming from the profitable blockade-running commerce. The Raineys set up shops for his barber business and her dressmaking in St. George and later Hamilton. After the Civil War ended, they returned to Georgetown where his commercial success and the need for black leadership in the Reconstruction South led to his varied and important career as a public servant.

First serving as the Republican Party chairman for Georgetown County, next he was chosen to represent Georgetown in the state's constitutional convention in 1868. Other active roles included agent for the state land commission, census taker, and brigadier general in the state militia. He attended the state labor convention supporting labor protection rights for African American workers to the General Assembly. His first elective office was as state senator from Georgetown, and he served as the chairman of the finance committee in 1870. In December of that year, he filled the unexpired term of Benjamin F. Whittemore, thus becoming the first black US Representative to the House. He was reelected four times serving until 1879, making history again in April 1874 when he became the first African American Speaker presiding over the House of Representatives.

Joseph H. Rainey, Joseph H. Rainy House, Georgetown
Wikimedia

His political career was marked by both his efforts to advance the interests of black people while also favoring a degree of leniency toward the whites. He supported an amnesty bill for former Confederates alleviating their debts and influenced the retention of a customs duty on rice, still a major export of his district and the state. He petitioned for funds to make improvements to Charleston Harbor and served on a committee for Invalid Pensions. His work on the Indian Affairs Committee sought antidiscrimination treatment for American Indians as well as Asian immigrants seeking entry to the United States.

But his work to establish and protect the rights of black citizens was the focus of his political career. On April 1, 1871, he gave a speech calling for federal troops to protect blacks from Ku Klux Klan terrorism. Shortly thereafter he received a letter threatening that he and other black civil rights advocates should "prepare to meet your God." The Ku Klux Klan Act passed but funding was blocked preventing enforcement. Rainey also supported public school desegregation, which was included in the Civil Rights Act of 1875, but it too was not enforced as the Reconstruction Era waned, so that desegregation and other civil rights for black Americans was not addressed again until decades later.

After leaving Congress, Joseph Rainey was appointed an agent for the Internal Revenue Service in South Carolina (1878–1881). He returned to an entrepreneurial life investing in railroads in Greenville and Columbia. He was a director of the Enterprise Railroad, a black-owned, horse-drawn railway that moved freight between the wharves and the railroad depot in Charleston. After an unsuccessful banking and brokerage business venture in Washington, DC, he returned to Georgetown where he died in 1887 and was buried in the Baptist Cemetery. The house on Prince Street in Georgetown is noted as the birthplace and childhood home of Joseph H. Rainey.

St. James-Santee Episcopal Church
Old Georgetown Road, Santee; 843-887-4386; stjamesec.org; services on Sunday at 10:00 a.m. (except on the second Sunday of Easter, which is held at The Chapel of Ease in McClellanville)

Alone in the back wilderness of the Lowcountry south of Georgetown sits a small but precious architectural treasure that dates from about 1768. This unlikely discovery in this rural setting is almost disorienting. But it makes an eloquent testimony to the power and importance of religion in colonial South Carolina. This Anglican parish was made up of area plantation owners whose wealth and political power were of great interest to the Church of England. Thus, churches like this were built in the hinterlands to make it "easy" for parishioners to worship and tithe in their rural settings. These satellite churches were called "chapels of ease."

Amazingly, several of these churches have survived, but none is more haunting and authentic than St. James-Santee Episcopal Church (The Brick Church) in this unusual and unexpected setting. The church itself has two classical porticoes, each supported by four brick Doric columns. If you are lucky, the church may be open, and you can see the high-backed, boxed pews separated by a cross axis of clay tile

St. James-Santee Episcopal Church
Wikimedia

St. James-Santee Episcopal Church—Interior
Wikimedia

flooring. The pews have never been painted. Look up to see the vaulted ceiling, which retains the original plaster dating from 1768. Only the pulpit is a modern replacement, and the general ambiance of this little chapel is overwhelmingly romantic. St. James-Santee Episcopal Church seems to generate its own will to survive. During the Civil War the chapel's communion silver was stolen, but after the war it was quietly returned. Vandals and vagrants have come and gone, but, by some miracle, the building looks the same today as it did when it was the center of religious thought for the plantation families living on the Santee Delta. Even the road to get there (once known as the King's Highway) is a sandy path that is nearly impassible in rainy weather. This sandy path was the main thoroughfare running north and south during colonial times. In fact, George Washington even passed through here on his presidential tour to the southern states in 1791. The entire landscape seems arrested in time.

To find the church from Charleston, drive north on US 17 toward Georgetown. Turn left on SC 857 (Rutledge Road). After passing Hampton Plantation State Park on the right, travel another mile and turn left on the sandy road. St. James-Santee Episcopal Church will be on the right. (While you are in the area, don't miss Hampton Plantation; see above.)

St. Stephen's Episcopal Church
196 State Rd. S-8-122 (Brick Church Circle), St. Stephen; 843-567-3419; Sunday services

First a bit of geography: St. Stephen's Parish was carved out of the original St. James-Santee Episcopal Parish (1706) centered around Jamestown just north of Charleston. Many French Huguenots who had come to South Carolina to escape religious and political oppression had settled in the lower Santee area in the early 1700s but learned that frequent flooding was a problem for their crops there. So many families moved upriver to higher ground and prospered as indigo planters. The English planters followed suit and soon predominated the area. The lower part of the parish became known as "French Santee" and the upper part, "English Santee." In 1754 English Santee officially split off and became St. Stephen's Parish, and the existing chapel of ease known as St. James-Santee Episcopal Church in Echaw fell within the new boundary. It then became known as St. Stephen's Church.

The old wooden chapel was in disrepair and did not reflect the prosperity and status of the area planters. Earlier in 1745 the British had placed a bounty on indigo, which was used, among other purposes, to dye cloth their Royal navy blue. This bounty turned indigo into a lucrative cash crop and quickly raised the fortunes of the indigo planters. The parishioners decided to build a new church and were diligent in demanding high-quality workmanship and materials. But as sometimes happens

St. Stephen's Episcopal Church, St. Stephen
Tina E. Mayland

when a committee is involved, decisions slowed the progress of construction. It is commonly believed that Francis Villepontoux and A. Howard whose names are engraved in exterior bricks were the architects, but some think some of the architectural plan may indicate otherwise. The church vestry and commissioners may have collaborated on the overall design; architectural purists point to the scale of the roof being too massive for the structure and the chancel window too small. The construction process was stymied several times when the bricks supplied by a vestry member were turned down a year later and even a second order of 150,000 bricks in 1764 from one of the commissioners were deemed "Entirely too Bad and are not Proper for Building a Church." Finally, the third time was the charm, and another commissioner's bricks passed scrutiny and were said to be "equal ... to Mr. Zachary

St. Stephen's Episcopal Church, St. Stephen
Tina E. Mayland

Villepontouxs" (known for his excellent brick supplied for St. Michael's Church and Pompion Hill Chapel; see Charleston & the Surrounding Area chapter).

Despite these setbacks the church was completed in 1767 after ten long years, and one account described it as "one of the handsomest country churches in South Carolina." Church records indicate that F. Villepontoux (nephew of Zachariah) and W. Axson were paid for brick and woodwork, and their skilled workmanship and the work of their enslaved labor force has stood the test of time. Axson had carved the intricate pulpit at Pompion Hill near Huger, and the canopied pulpit here is remarkably similar, if less decorated. The showstopper is the reredos or panel framing the altar. Three gilded sunbursts symbolizing God's grace adorn the dark wood paneling and are framed by the classical entablature supported by fluted pilasters. The central Palladian window is flanked by tablets containing text of the Apostles' Creed and the Lord's Prayer. Axson not only left his name and Masonic marks on an exterior brick, just above it is a brick that appears to depict a man in a pulpit, perhaps to claim his building of the one inside.

The tall gambrel roof accommodates a cove ceiling like one in St. Michael's Church, the new standard for proper Anglican ecclesiastical structures. A bull's eye window dots each of the curvilinear baroque gable ends of the roof. The rectangular building has the typical central north, west, and south entrances with flanking arched windows. These are neatly separated by Doric brick pilasters rising to a wide wooden cornice at the roof line, lending the order and symmetry desired by 18th-century sensibilities. After the Revolution the population declined and the parish church fell into decline, but fortunately several renovations over the decades kept the building intact. Today, services have resumed with regular Sunday morning services.

Snow's Island
East of Johnsonville; Florence County; privately owned

General Francis Marion, one of the most famous heroes of the American Revolution, was largely famous for being remarkably hard to find. He is said to be the "inventor" of modern guerilla warfare. The British fought in conventional ways on battlefields and on horseback; by contrast, Marion chose to encounter his enemy in wooded swamps and dense backwaters, which gave him the advantage of surprise attack. The elusiveness of his tactics meant that he had to stay constantly on the move so the British could not find and stop this astonishingly successful band of ragtag rebels.

One National Historic Landmark in a swampy area along the Pee Dee River in Florence County attempts to represent the environment that spawned the heroic deeds of the "Swamp Fox" and his brave followers. As British commander Sir Banastre Tarleton so aptly put it, "the devil himself . . . could not catch this damned old fox." For four months from December 1780 to March 1781, Marion used Snow's Island as his base of operations. It was an ideal hidden location on a river plateau accessible only by water since all bridges had been destroyed; Marion stored supplies, plotted attacks, and rested his men here.

On March 29 a British force of 300 New York Volunteers under Lt. Colonel Welborn E. Doyle dedicated to finding the elusive general searched and finally found Marion's base camp. Marion was fighting elsewhere but had left a small contingent to guard the supplies. Colonel Hugh Ervin of Marion's militia quickly destroyed their precious supplies and ammunition by tossing much of it into the river as Doyle advanced upon them. Greatly outnumbered, Ervin and his band fled but seven of his men were killed and 15 captured in the action. In addition, Doyle destroyed the camp, and it was subsequently abandoned by Marion and his men. But he continued his guerilla tactics and along with other more conventional warfare by Patriot generals, these engagements contributed significantly to the defeat of the British Southern Campaign leading up to the surrender at Yorktown.

This same elusiveness outlived Marion's lifetime and continued through the annals of history until he all but disappeared. He was pushed back further into obscurity when famous artists created memorable battle images of Washington, Tarleton, and Cornwallis. More recent film portrayals of the Swamp Fox by the likes of Leslie Nielson and Mel Gibson have brought back some attention to his story;

Snow's Island Swamp Fox
Lee Davis Perry

as his gravesite promises: "History will record . . . his memory as one of the most distinguished Patriots and heroes of the American Revolution."

Even though the Snow's Island site is not accessible to the public, glimpses of General Francis Marion can, in fact, be found in a trail of outdoor murals displayed in a number of small towns in Clarendon County. His likeness appears on the outer wall of banks, shopping centers, and grocery stores. In all, 22 murals by different contemporary artists have resurrected scenes from Marion's life and military career. When seen in aggregate, they create a rare, three-dimensional portrait of the famous Swamp Fox from South Carolina. Visit www.swampfoxtrail.com for details on locations and guided tours.

Chapter 4
THE FALL LINE

Borough House
SC Hwy. 261, N. Kings Hwy., Stateburg; 803-757-0425; borough house.com; limited access

Across the highway from the historic Church of the Holy Cross (see below) is the complex of buildings that make up Borough House Plantation. The property records date back to 1758 when a tavern/house was located there. It is believed that the Borough House name came from the fact that it was the only house in the early settlement of Stateborough or Stateburg as it came to be known. The property is also referred to as Anderson Place and Hillcrest Plantation too. At different times during the Revolutionary War, both Continental Army General Nathanael Greene and British General Lord Cornwallis set up their military headquarters on-site due to its central location on the King's Highway, a major thoroughfare at the time.

Borough House, Stateburg
Courtesy Library of Congress

Dr. William Wallace Anderson added wings to the main house in 1821. The additions were built of rammed earth walls or *pisé de terre* as were 6 other outbuildings on the plantation. This non-traditional building material was made by compacting earth between forms to construct walls. It is an ancient technique used by the Babylonians dating back to 5000 BC and also the Chinese for sections of The Great Wall. A stucco coating protected the exterior from moisture, and the walls proved to be extremely durable. Dr. Anderson's labor force was made up of his enslaved African Americans who built the buildings as well as worked his cotton plantation. This collection of structures is the largest grouping of high style *pisé de terre* buildings in the United States. Dr. Anderson was also instrumental in convincing the vestry of the Church of the Holy Cross to build their church with rammed earth later in 1850.

Two other events during Dr. Anderson's ownership of Borough House Plantation have significance in our national history. On October 7, 1821, Richard H. Anderson was born to Dr. Anderson and his wife, Mary Jane Mackensie Anderson. Their son was to grow up to become a general in the Confederate Army, "Fighting Dick" Anderson. Also, while visiting Dr. Anderson in 1851, Joel Roberts Poinsett, statesman, diplomat, and botanist, died and was buried in the churchyard of Church of the Holy Cross across the road.

During the Civil War Union Colonel George Potter spared the house from burning when he learned that Elizabeth Anderson, Dr. Anderson's second wife, who owned the house after her husband's death in 1864, was a member of the Eastern Star. This was the women's Masonic group and Potter was a Mason. The plantation was plundered but left standing.

Other notable history of the property was when then owner Mary Virginia Saunders White converted the cotton plantation to a timber managed tree farm in 1946. Certificate #1 was issued by the South Carolina Tree Farms System since it was the first of its kind in the state. Borough House Plantation is still privately owned and managed by Anderson family descendants today.

Camden Battlefield
1606 Flat Rock Rd., Camden; (803) 432-9841; historiccamden.org; open daily year-round; free

It is not widely known that more Revolutionary battles and skirmishes (245 of them) were fought in South Carolina than any other colony. In fact, most of the war was fought right here. The Camden area, 30 miles north of Columbia off of I–20, is the ideal place to trace some of the action and events.

Camden, established in 1732, is the oldest inland town in the state. The Historic Camden Revolutionary War Site, located at 222 Broad St., is a 107-acre outdoor museum complex and is the site of the original town of Camden, which was taken

Camden Battlefield, Camden
Historic Camden Foundation

and fortified by the British in 1780. Portions of the palisade walls have been rebuilt where they originally stood. The old mansion, built earlier on the site by Joseph Kershaw, one of the town fathers, was used as British headquarters by General Cornwallis during the occupation and has been reconstructed. You can explore the Historic Camden Revolutionary War Site on your own for a general admission fee. Or you may book a guided interactive tour offered Tuesday through Sunday for an additional fee.

The Camden Battlefield covers 476 acres of the core battlefield and is located about eight miles north of the Broad Street campus at 1606 Flat Rock Rd. By 1780 Camden was the largest city outside of Charles Town (present-day Charleston) and was the economic and cultural heart of the North and South Carolina backcountry. After capturing Charles Town earlier in 1780, General Cornwallis located his garrison and main supply post in Camden serving all the British military operations in the South. Strategically, it was important both to the British Army that occupied it, and the Americans who wanted it back. After a series of mistakes before and during the Battle of Camden, the Patriots under Major General Horatio Gates were soundly defeated. Suffering heavy casualties, the Americans retreated in disarray. Captured soldiers were held and some were executed by the British in their fortified town. But the disastrous defeat led to changes in leadership that changed the course

Battle of Camden Historic Marker
Historic Camden Foundation

SOUTH   CAROLINA

BATTLE OF CAMDEN

Near here on August 16, 1780, an
American army under General Gates
was defeated by British forces
commanded by Lord Cornwallis.
Major General Baron de Kalb was
mortally wounded in this battle.

BRITISH TROOPS ENGAGED

Tarleton's Legion, Twenty-third, Thirty-third and Seventy-first Regiments,
Volunteers of Ireland, Royal Artillery, four light infantry companies,
Royal North Carolina Militia, volunteer militia, and pioneers.

AMERICAN TROOPS ENGAGED

Armand's Legion, First and Second Maryland Brigades, Delaware
Regiment, First Artillery Regiment, Porterfield's Light Infantry,
North Carolina Militia, and Virginia Militia.

of the war. Among them, Major General Nathanael Greene was placed in charge of the Southern Campaign. The two major battles fought here—the Battle of Camden (1780) and the smaller Battle of Hobkirk Hill (1781)—contributed to British General Cornwallis's retreat north and his eventual surrender to Washington at Yorktown, Virginia, in October 1781. For its role in our nation's founding, the battlefield was designated a National Historic Landmark in 1961.

The battlefield has three miles of walking trails with interpretive signage and is free to walk around during daylight hours. Just remember no metal detecting, digging, or camping is allowed. A monthly guided tour is available for a fee and includes the Historic Site admission as well.

Chapelle Administration Building
Allen University, 1530 Harden St., Columbia; 803-376-5700; allenuniversity.edu; weekdays year round

"To teach the mind to think, the heart to love, and the hands to work" was the goal of one of the early leaders of Allen University that carries forward to its mission today. Allen had its beginnings as Payne Institute in Cokesbury, SC, founded in 1870 by the African Methodist Episcopal Church (AME). Its objective was to educate black clergy during a period of suppression in the Reconstruction Era. After ten years Bishop William F. Dickerson spearheaded a move to Columbia, a more central and vibrant location for expanding the school, and land was purchased for $6,000. It was renamed Allen University in honor of Bishop Richard Allen who founded the AME Church and received a charter from the state on December 20, 1880. Under the leadership of the first two presidents, J. E. Walters and J. W. Morris, the university established the theological and law departments and made great strides. Enrollment was made up of students from South Carolina, other nearby states, and the Caribbean, and by the end of the decade seventy-five graduates held degrees from the Normal Collegiate, Law, and Theological departments.

Another dynamic president, David Henry Sims, grew the opportunities at Allen, which now also had instruction in classical, scientific, English, music, and industrial studies. Sims started a faculty exchange program with Benedict College located nearby and both schools participated in joint summer school. Leading up to the Great Depression, classes were held for elementary and high school students as well, bringing total enrollment to 1,780. Despite Sims's best efforts the university struggled financially, just as so many other educational institutions did at the time. Post–World War II, an influx of veterans revived the school and departments of Humanities, Philosophy, and Psychology were added to the offerings.

One building stands out on Allen University's campus for several reasons: its design by a noted architect, and the black leaders to attend and congregate there.

Allen University, Chappelle Administration Building
Wikimedia

The Chappelle Administration Building (also spelled Chapelle in some sources) was built from 1922–1925 in the Colonial Revival style. John Anderson Lankford (1874–1946), considered the "dean of black architects," created a 3½-story stately structure with a cupola centered over the 14-bay width of the red-brick façade. The slate roof has five gabled dormer windows, and stone keystones and garland panels decorate the windows on the first and second floors. Another pleasing feature is the triple-arched porch framing the central doorway and its flanking windows. It housed a dining hall, kitchen, administrative offices, auditorium, and classroom space as it still does today. This structure cost a staggering $165,000 to build and is one of Lankford's most significant works.

Lankford rose from a modest background in Patosi, Missouri, to study and receive degrees at Lincoln Institute (now Lincoln University) and later Tuskegee Institute at the invitation of Booker T. Washington. His career took him to several universities, mainly African American schools, where he both taught courses in mechanical engineering and refined his skills. His accomplished reputation spread as he designed buildings around the southeast. After moving to Washington, DC, Lankford's plans were chosen for the United Order of True Reformers Hall, the first project in the nation that was financed, designed, and erected solely by blacks in 1903. He designed fashionable residences for leading black professionals in DC,

Virginia, and Maryland, but his passion was building black churches "as a simple and common duty to our church, our race, and to our God." In 1908 he was appointed the Chief Architect of the African Methodist Episcopal Church. In this capacity he designed the Chappelle Building named for Bishop William D. Chappelle, Allen University president, 1898–1899.

The 7,300-square-foot auditorium contained within the building has hosted many notables including Dr. Martin Luther King Jr., Mary McLeod Bethune, Muhammed Ali, Rev. Jesse Jackson, and US Senator Strom Thurmond. It was the site of meetings to organize efforts for school integration leading up to the US Supreme Court case, *Brown v. Board of Education* in 1954. Nationally known performers including Leontyne Price and Langston Hughes appeared on the stage here.

Distinguished Allen graduates include civil rights advocate J. A. DeLaine, SC state legislators Senator Kay Patterson and Senator Clementa Pinckney, and the first African American president of AARP, Dr. Margaret Dixon. The first African American president of the South Carolina Education Association and South Carolina's Teacher of the Year, Dr. Agnes H. W. Burgess, numerous college and university presidents, and a dozen bishops of the AME Church add to the prominent alumni list. The building underwent a $3 million interior renovation in 2015 and has maintained its historic integrity and function of the original design.

Church of the Holy Cross
335 N. Kings Hwy., SC Hwy. 261, Stateburg; 803-494-8101; holycrossstateburg.com; limited access

Church of the Holy Cross is an Anglican church located in the region called the High Hills of Santee near Sumter, South Carolina, in the town of Stateburg. Stateburg was founded in 1783 by Revolutionary War hero General Thomas Sumter who hoped it would become the state capital. About this time the South Carolina General Assembly had decided to relocate the capital from Charleston to a central part of the state. Stateburg just missed becoming the capital by a few votes to a place called Granby on the Congaree River near Columbia. Frequent flooding later caused another move across the river to higher ground in Columbia, which continues as the state capital.

Originally, an earlier church, Episcopal Church of Claremont, was built on the Stateburg site on land donated by Thomas Sumter. This church was an outreach of St. Mark's Episcopal Church in Pinewood, SC. A group of parishioners of St. Mark's petitioned for a chapel of ease so that they would not have to travel some distance to Pinewood. The state legislature granted them a charter in 1788 to build their own church on the donated land. To raise funds for erecting it, the pews were sold individually and deeded to the highest bidder.

Church of the Holy Cross, Stateburg
Joe Perry

By 1847 the wooden church needed replacing and a prominent Charleston architect, Edward C. Jones, was hired to design a Victorian Gothic church in a cruciform plan to be named Church of the Holy Cross. The Building Committee led by Dr. William Wallace Anderson convinced the vestry to construct the church in *pisé de terre* or rammed earth. This material consists of several layers of earth compacted between forms to make a wall. The lower cost for the walls versus other more traditional materials, he persuaded, would allow for a larger church to be built. The church's cornerstone was laid September 11, 1850, and it was consecrated two years later by the Right Reverend Francis Huger Rutledge, Bishop of Florida.

The Church of the Holy Cross is thought to be the finest example of rammed earth construction in the United States as well as an exceptionally beautiful illustration of Victorian High Gothic Revival design. Its walls stand 40 feet tall and are 18 to 22 inches thick. To protect them from the elements, a stucco coating mixture of clay, sand, lime, and pebbles was applied with brooms to the exterior. The walls and buttresses support a steeply pitched tile roof. A bell tower rises at one end with Gothic arched windows and doors punctuating the structure. On the inside, lath and plaster coat the walls painted to resemble stone blocks. An oak leaf frieze decorates the top of the walls, and the highly vaulted ceilings provide a framework for the luminous trio of stained-glass windows in the chancel. These windows were made in Bavaria after the designs of Eugene Viollet-le-Duc, a noted French architect. The church also contains an Erben organ, one of the few extant in the United States. Constructed by the renowned organ maker Henry Erben, it was installed in 1851 and has received almost continuous use since that time.

The churchyard contains many notables worth visiting. Two of them are the graves of Joel R. Poinsett, statesman, physician, diplomat, and botanist who introduced the "poinsettia" to America, and George L. Mabry Jr., Major General, US Army, and Medal of Honor Recipient. After an extensive renovation the church was re-consecrated in 2010, and an active congregation worships there today.

First Baptist Church
1306 Hampton St., Columbia; 803-256-4251; fbccola.com; limited access

Call it "divine intervention" or maybe just pure luck but the First Baptist Church in downtown Columbia narrowly escaped the flames of Union forces on their rampage of retribution in the final days of the Civil War. By the end of 1864, Union General William T. Sherman had embarked on his "March to the Sea," burning and plundering his way through Georgia. With the beginning of the new year, Sherman and his troops left Savannah, turning back north with the goal of inflicting even greater destruction on the people of the Palmetto State, the instigators of secession and armed rebellion. They first took Columbia by firing upon it from across the

First Baptist Church, Columbia
Wikimedia

Congaree River damaging many buildings including the walls of the State House, which was under construction at the time. (See South Carolina State House below.) The invading soldiers, who had been turned loose on the city, ignited fires that ultimately burned over one-third of the buildings in February 1865. Determined to locate the church where the seeds of secession had been sown, they consulted the First Baptist Church custodian, a black man who pointed them to the Washington Street Methodist Church, which they promptly burned, thus sparing First Baptist.

The James Petigru Boyce Chapel was the second First Baptist Church building erected in 1859 funded by James P. Boyce, former pastor of the church and first president of the Southern Baptist Theological Seminary. Ironically, Boyce was opposed to secession and ran as an anti-secession candidate to the Secession Convention of December 1860. He was defeated but later aligned himself with the Confederacy, serving as a chaplain, state legislator, and aide to Governor Andrew Magrath, ascending to the rank of lieutenant colonel.

The Secession Convention took place on December 17, 1860, at the Boyce Chapel of the First Baptist Church. The SC General Assembly had previously met in November to vote for presidential electors and remained in Columbia to ascertain the election results. When Lincoln was declared the winner, they immediately called for an election of state delegates to attend a special state convention centrally located in Columbia. This election of representatives by the people of the state largely consisted of pro-secession planters and political leaders who came together for the convention held at the church. The vote was taken for South Carolina to secede from the Union and was unanimous at 169–0. It was the only unanimous vote among the other southern states that later decided to secede. Due to an outbreak of smallpox, the convention adjourned in Columbia and reconvened in Charleston on December 20. Here they made it official by signing South Carolina's Ordinance of Secession, exercising what they believed was a state's right to leave the union and putting in motion a joining together of other southern states that would form the Confederate States of America, and ultimately a terrible divisive conflict between the North and the South.

The small brick building has undergone several renovations and additions over the years. It has retained its Tuscan brick pilasters and columns supporting the sizeable pediment all in a Greek Revival style. It remains a part of the First Baptist Church campus of buildings bounded by Hampton, Sumter, Washington, and Marion Streets, all serving an active congregation originally established in 1809.

Graniteville Historic District
SC Hwy. 19 (Canal Street), Church, Gregg, Marshall, and Taylor
Streets, Graniteville; privately owned

Thankfully, most visionaries tend to ignore the naysayers of their time bringing us new ideas and new ways of doing things. William Gregg was one such man who made a big impact on the economic future of South Carolina. Gregg first had a highly successful career as a Charleston jeweler, and, after touring the textile mills of New England, he determined that the predominantly agrarian antebellum South needed to industrialize to be economically competitive. He bought up land in the lower Edgefield District near Aiken from which he planned to quarry granite and cut timber for his new factory. He must have been quite persuasive as he obtained financial backing from Charleston businessmen of $300,000 to start a model textile business on Horse Creek, receiving a charter for the Graniteville Company in 1845.

After four years of construction of a canal for waterpower and a mill building outfitted with the latest spinning and weaving equipment, the mill began operating in 1849. It was said to be "more modern than many of its New England contemporaries." One hundred worker houses, a schoolhouse, stores, and two churches completed his vision of the ideal mill town. Gregg supervised not only the construction of the entire village, but also the moral behavior of his employees by forbidding alcohol consumption and dancing, requiring all workers' children to attend his free school, and refusing to hire any children under 12 years old. Another unusual and controversial tactic was his employment of white laborers, mostly women and teenage children, instead of the more common practice in southern factories of using an enslaved labor force.

After a slow start, the Graniteville Company prospered manufacturing cotton shirting and sheeting and selling to markets around the country. Profits saw a return of up to 18 percent for investors by 1854. Gregg's dictums that the South was ripe for industrialization due to abundant water sources for power, proximity to high quality cotton, and a cheap labor force were now shown to be true. One textile historian said of him, he "not only preached the gospel of industrialization, he took practical steps to realize it." His success influenced the spread of other cotton mills around the South. As the Civil War approached, Gregg signed the South Carolina Ordinance of Secession and was named president of the Manufacturing and Direct Trade Association of the Confederacy. The mill went into full production producing cloth for uniforms and other materials for the southern cause.

It escaped major damage during the war and expanded into other markets in the following decades. Two factories were built in Vaucluse and Warrenville nearby, and two were purchased in Augusta, GA. Due to increased competition and later the Great Depression, the company experienced some periods of financial strain.

Gregg Street, Graniteville Mills Home
Wikimedia

But World War I and World War II pulled profits back up as government contracts came in. This allowed for modernization of the mill and innovation as a pioneer in permanent press fabric production. The company continues operation today as Graniteville Specialty Fabrics.

The Graniteville Historic District is made up of the 1846 Graniteville Canal, the 1849 Graniteville Mill, 26 of the original workers' houses plus additional mill housing, the 1847 Graniteville Academy, and the 1849 St. John's Methodist Church covering 55 acres. The 2½ story mill building was constructed with local blue granite with three entry towers capped with cupolas, one of which had a bell for summoning employees to work. Most of the village structures were designed in the Early Gothic Revival style with steeply pitched roofs and white board and batten siding on red brick foundations. The district is a visual representation of the start and large-scale expansion of the textile industry in South Carolina and throughout the South.

Millford Plantation
7320 Millford Plantation Rd., SC Hwy. 261, Pinewood;
classicalamericanhomes.org; limited access; admission charge

Tucked into the area called "The High Hills of Santee," Millford Plantation often takes visitors by surprise when they discover this highly sophisticated, monumental architectural gem in the hilly backwoods of the state. Its remote location is about ninety miles northwest of Charleston and forty-five miles southeast of Columbia, perhaps contributing to its mystique. Sometimes referred to as "Manning's Folly," the

Millford Plantation, Pinewood
Lee Davis Perry

grand home was built by John Laurence Manning (later governor of South Carolina 1852–54) and his wife, Susan Frances Hampton Manning, when they were both only 22 years old. Manning had been given the land by his grandparents, and, most likely, Susan Hampton Manning's inherited wealth paid for the house to be built. She was the daughter of Wade Hampton I, the richest man in South Carolina, if not the South. Among her assets was a share of the sizable profits from a sugar cane plantation in Louisiana called Houmas Plantation. Nearly a thousand enslaved African Americans toiled to make it extremely productive during a peak time for sugar cane prices in 1840. Since no major farming took place in the sandy soil of Millford, it is assumed that sugar cane was the revenue source. The extravagant home was believed to be influenced by Susan's brother, Wade Hampton II, who built a similar home with the same builder, Nathaniel Potter, called "Millwood" on the site of their father's home closer to Columbia. One can only imagine the fabulous entertaining that must have taken place at the young couple's showplace before the war intervened.

Millford narrowly escaped burning during the final days of the Civil War unlike its equally grand counterpart, Millwood. Millwood was burned to the ground by General Sherman's troops. As later owner Richard Jenrette said, divine providence must have intervened. Northern troops commanded by General Edward. E. Potter arrived on April 19, 1865, before news of the surrender at Appomatox on April 9

Milford Plantation Interior, Pinewood
Lee Davis Perry

reached Millford. Governor Manning "greeted" him at the front door. When he heard the General's name, he reportedly said, "This house was built by a Potter, and I suppose it will be destroyed by a Potter." General Potter replied "No, you are protected." It turned out that the general was related to Nathaniel Potter, the architect and builder of Millford from Rhode Island. Millford was spared from destruction that day but not from the long, trying years of Reconstruction and economic hardship to follow in South Carolina.

The Manning family managed to hold onto the property until 1902 when it was sold to Mary Clark Thompson, a wealthy New Yorker. She bought Millford as a winter and hunting retreat for her family and passed it on to her Clark nephews. Under the Clark family's stewardship over the next ninety years, Millford was lovingly refurbished, erasing the decay of the post–Civil War period. In 1992 Richard Hampton Jenrette purchased the mansion and surrounding 400 acres while the Clarks retained the adjoining 2,500 acres. Jenrette, a Wall Street investment banker and a well-respected historic preservationist, wanted to add to his collection of classical architectural homes around the country and Millford fit the bill. He considered it "the finest extant example of Greek Revival residential architecture in America," and most architectural historians agree.

Fortunately, "Aunt Mary" had insisted that the original furnishings should convey with the house so that when Jenrette purchased it, the late–Duncan Phyfe made furniture was still on-site albeit stored in the attic, hallways, and barn. Accompanying bills of sale from D. Phyfe & Son, New York, document the purchase by Governor Manning in 1840–43. Jenrette had the furniture cleaned, polished, and reupholstered in new blue and gold silk fabric, reinstalling it back in the magnificent double parlors of the house. The custom-made white marble mantels from Philadelphia and their large, gilt-frame mirrors above were brought by ship to Charleston then by barge up the Santee River, not only amazingly surviving an arduous journey but also another 160 years of use. Jenrette purchased two large Waterford chandeliers c. 1840 and commissioned classical motif Scalamandré carpets to complete the stunningly beautiful rooms. The stained-glass oculus in the domed ceiling of the curved staircase and the elegant woodwork around original mahogany doors with their silver locks and tall windows with original panes of wavy glass speak to the fine finishes throughout the house. No wonder Jenrette called Millford his "Taj Mahal."

Richard H. Jenrette left Millford Plantation, as well as five other incredible historic homes (see Robert William Roper House in Charleston & the Surrounding Area chapter) that he painstakingly preserved under the stewardship of the Classical American Homes Preservation Trust, leaving a legacy of some of America's finest classical art and architecture. He hoped that generations to come might have an immersive experience in American history by visiting these sites to contemplate and learn from our country's past.

Robert Mills House
1616 Blanding St., Columbia; 803-252-7742; historiccolumbia.org;
open Tues through Sun; admission charged

Under the auspices of the Historic Columbia Foundation is the impressive Robert
Mills House and Gardens at 1616 Blanding St. Robert Mills is the architect who
designed the Washington Monument in our nation's capital, among other important
landmarks in Columbia and around South Carolina.

Mills was born in 1781 and raised in Charleston and is considered America's
first professional architect. He was invited by Thomas Jefferson to stay at Monticello
and study Jefferson's large, personal collection of architectural books for two years.
He also studied under James Hoban, designer of the White House, and Benjamin
Henry Latrobe, the leading architect of the new nation from whom he gained knowledge and appreciation for the Classical Revival style. His early career was spent in
Philadelphia designing churches and other professional organization structures such
as Washington Hall and a refurbishing of Independence Hall.

In 1814 he relocated to Baltimore where he designed the first Washington Monument, which was scaled back due to budget constraints to a statue atop a large, single
column supported by a plinth. After many commissions for government to include
buildings and renovations for the US Treasury, Patent Office, Post Office, and Capitol, he subsequently won the competition for the DC Washington Monument. It

Robert Mills House, Columbia
Wikimedia

originally was planned to have a circular colonnaded museum of American culture with a roadway leading up to a platform for viewing the central massive masonry obelisk. Financial restrictions again eliminated all but the obelisk on the Mall, yet it remains an iconic landmark nevertheless.

In South Carolina Robert Mills is most remembered for his work as Superintendent of Public Buildings in the state. He was commissioned to build twelve jails, sixteen courthouses, and the (then called) South Carolina Lunatic Asylum in Columbia (see Mills Building, South Carolina State Hospital below). The design of the County Record Building or Fireproof Building in Charleston (see Charleston & the Surrounding Area chapter) was updated to utilize colonial Palladian layout with more durable masonry vaulted construction, thus the "fireproof" designation.

The Robert Mills House, originally called the Ainsley Hall House, is named for its designer but was originally built for Ainsley and Sarah Hall in 1823. But thereafter the Classical Revival mansion came into use by a series of different religious schools including Columbia Bible College and a Presbyterian theological seminary. Eventually it fell into disrepair and was slated for demolition in 1960, until local preservation-minded advocates formed Historic Columbia Foundation to save the early 19th-century architectural treasure.

Today, the Foundation operates it as museum house and gardens with the ground floor housing its shop and ticket office. A tour of the house features period rooms with late 18th- through mid-19th decorative arts. The Hampton-Preston Mansion and Gardens, the Mann-Simons Site, and the Woodrow Wilson Family Home are the other three Historic Columbia museum houses in the Robert Mills Historic District and a combination ticket for two, three, or all four houses is offered.

Mills Building, South Carolina State Hospital
2100 Bull St., Columbia; privately owned; limited access

Another South Carolina building designed by Robert Mills (see above), the State Hospital, or South Carolina Lunatic Asylum as it was originally called, was both innovative in design and purpose. In the early 19th-century treatment of the mentally ill consisted of locking people away in prison-like, inhumane settings. A small group of local doctors, lawyers, and legislators, influenced by new ideas from England and France, sought to create an environment for curative and humane treatment for all societal classes. The General Assembly passed an act in 1821 that authorized construction of a state hospital specifically for this purpose, establishing it as only the third state mental institution of its kind in the country. Due to various delays the building was not completed until 1827, opening for patients in 1828.

The asylum nearly closed after only a few years because it was unable to attract enough paying patients. Fees generated from the wealthier patients were supposed to

Mills Building, South Carolina State Hospital, Columbia
Wikimedia

cover them while also subsidizing the poorer ones, and county funds were supposed to cover the indigent. With a patient count never more than 200 through the 1860s, the state had to lend financial support to keep the hospital operating. Initially only serving white patients, another act in 1849 allowed both enslaved and free blacks admission but few came there before the Civil War.

Due to extensive poverty in South Carolina after the war, indigent patient admissions increased dramatically. The state began covering the costs for the poor or "beneficiary" patients, and their numbers continued to grow. By 1900 they numbered over 1,000, rising to 2,000 by 1920, of which nearly half were African American, and most were beneficiaries. Although admissions were up, care and conditions at the hospital deteriorated. Renamed the South Carolina State Hospital for the Insane, it largely abandoned its curative mission, instead becoming a custodial institution for chronic and incurable cases. Lack of funding and other administrative problems led to unsanitary conditions and a high mortality rate, especially among blacks. After legislative investigations Governor Richard I. Manning was instrumental in setting up major reforms in 1915 to address the issues. This helped to bring down the death rate but overcrowding and underfunding were ongoing struggles for the hospital.

Additions to the Mills's building as well as new buildings on the grounds attempted to alleviate the crowding as well as provide for a nursing school. By 1930 black patients were transferred to a separate facility located several miles away; this lasted until the desegregation movement of the 1960s when it became a geriatric care facility. The Depression and World War II years saw another large influx of patients reaching almost 4,000 residents by the 1950s, again creating significant problems for adequate care. Various developments in the mental health field over the next decades such as community care, new therapeutics, and Medicaid led to a gradual decline in institutional admissions, and the South Carolina State Hospital followed this trend. It closed its doors to patients, serving only as offices for the Department of Mental Health and later the Department of Health & Environmental Control.

Robert Mills's thoughtful and innovative design was cutting edge at the time. He wanted the structure to combine "elegancy with permanency, economy and security from fire." It was largely constructed with stone, brick, and cast iron, making it fire resistant. The exterior is true to Mills's classical Greek Revival designs with a central section flanked by two angled side wings on an arcaded high basement. Windows are rounded at the top on the first level or flat topped above, and all have stone lintels. The entrance is covered by a large, pedimented portico supported with six massive Doric columns. Curving granite steps are used in the front with a half-round turret stair tower attached in the rear, extending from the ground all the way to the roof four stories high. At one point the roof supported a roof garden, believed to be the first of its kind.

On the interior Mills showed his concern for patient care with all rooms facing south for sunlight and fresh air, opening to a wide corridor for circulation. A cupola atop the roof also provided ventilation for the upper levels. A contemporary newspaper account reported that "Not the smallest appearance of a prison is manifest in the building. Security is agreeably under appearances familiar . . . in every private house . . . iron bars take the similitude of sashes; the hinges and locks of the doors are all secret; so that every temptation is put out of the way to make an escape . . ." The original appropriation for the building was $30,000 but ended up costing close to $100,000. A 2020 fire damaged part of the center structure, but private developers who now own the property have plans to renovate and protect.

Mulberry Plantation (James and Mary Boykin Chesnut House)
559 Sumter Hwy. (US Hwy. 521), Camden; privately owned

"I do not pretend to go to sleep. How can I? If Anderson does not accept terms at four o'clock, the orders are he shall be fired upon. I count four by St. Michael's chimes, and I begin to hope.

"At half past four, the heavy booming of a cannon! I sprang out of bed and on my knees, prostrate, I prayed as I never prayed before . . .

"I put on my double-gown and a shawl and went to the house top. The shells were bursting . . . I knew my husband was rowing about in a boat somewhere in

Mulberry Plantation, Camden
Wikimedia

that dark bay, and that the shells were roofing it over, bursting toward the Fort . . . The regular roar of the cannon, there it was! And who could tell what each volley accomplished of death and destruction."

It was April 12, 1861. Mary Boykin Chesnut was staying at the Planter's Hotel in Charleston, having accompanied her husband, James Chesnut Jr., to the hotbed of the sectional crisis. James was a member of Confederate General Pierre G. T. Beauregard's staff involved in the negotiations with Union commander Maj. Robert Anderson, occupying Fort Sumter in Charleston Harbor. As described in her diaries, Mary was an eyewitness to the unfolding drama, simultaneously feeling fear and excitement, as she well understood the ramifications of this terrible violence. The Confederate bombardment continued until the following afternoon when Anderson surrendered the fort. Miraculously, no lives were lost, and the South was jubilant in its expedient victory. All believed that the war would soon end. Of course, the divisive conflict did not end soon, nor would it take place without tremendous loss of life on both sides.

Mary Boykin Miller Chesnut was the daughter of South Carolina Governor Stephen Decatur Miller and Mary Boykin Miller, who raised her with all the advantages of wealth, social position, and education. At seventeen she married into another prominent family, the Chesnuts of Mulberry Plantation, located just a few miles south of Camden, where she led a privileged if "tedious" life largely made possible by the work of enslaved black workers. Mulberry was one of the largest and

Mulberry Plantation First Floor Stair Hall
Wikimedia

most prosperous inland cotton plantations of South Carolina, at one point covering 12,000 acres.

The main house was built c. 1820 in the Federal style befitting the prominence of the Chesnut family and may have had native South Carolina architect Robert Mills's input on the design. It is a large, 3½ story house with red brick walls composed of bricks made on-site by the enslaved craftspeople of Mulberry and laid in a Flemish bond pattern. Some of the fine interior and exterior finishes include dentil molding, fluted pilasters and columns, marble steps, wrought-iron railings, intricate woodwork, and silver doorknobs. The main significance of the house, however, is that it was the primary home of Mary Chesnut during the period of her collecting the material and writing her diaries. In them, she reveals her transition from critical comments about slavery and plantation life in the early days of the war to viewing Mulberry as a nostalgic symbol of all that the antebellum South had lost at the end.

During the war years, as the wife of a Confederate general then serving as advisor to President Jefferson Davis, Mary Boykin Chesnut found herself in an extraordinary position, often surrounded by the leadership of the South at important occasions where she more than held her own, impressing generals and politicians with her knowledge of military and governmental matters. She would follow firsthand the rise, short life, and demise of the Confederacy from the first shots at Fort Sumter, the formation of a government in Montgomery, Alabama, and the workings of the capital in Richmond, Virginia, to a bitter end back in her home state of South Carolina. "It was a way I had, always to stumble on the real show." Fortunately, she also directed this "way" into recording her experiences and compiling journals, insightfully describing the major players who shaped the events of this turbulent time.

Following the surrender, she and her husband returned to Mulberry, where the reality of starting over in a broken, unfamiliar world set in. "It is a wearisome thought; that late in life we are to begin anew, with laborious, difficult days ahead." Amid coping with rebuilding their lives after the war, Mary Chesnut managed to carve out time to revise and rework her journals in the hopes of their eventual publication. She did not live to see them in print, but her words live on in several edited versions of her forty-eight copybooks, which contained more than 2,500 pages. The first one is titled *A Diary from Dixie*, published in 1905, 19 years after her death. One biographer, Elisabeth Muhlenfeld, calls Mary's writings "in many respects the most remarkable firsthand account of the Confederacy ever written."

(Much earlier history from prehistoric times is being studied revealing an Indian village site on Mulberry lands. It is also believed to be the site of the Native American town called Cofitachiqui where Spanish explorer Hernando de Soto met their ruler, the "Lady of Cofitachiqui," in 1540.)

South Carolina State House
1100 Gervais St., Columbia; 803-734-2430; southcarolinastatehouse.com; open for guided or self-guided tours Mon through Sat; free

Travelers to South Carolina's capital city, Columbia, quickly notice that nearly all roads lead to the center of the city and converge at South Carolina's imposing Greek Revival State House. This crossroads of legislation and history has a background as romantic and dramatic as the state itself. Columbia's first state house, a wooden structure dating from 1790 was designed by James Hoban (designer of the White House.) By the 1850s South Carolina had outgrown the old state house, and plans were made to erect an impressive fireproof building to replace it. Work began on the new capitol building as early as 1851, but the architect who had been hired for the project became entangled in a controversy over fraudulent practices and was summarily fired. A new architect reworked the plans and construction began again in 1855. But the Civil War intervened and dramatically slowed the progress, and work was completely suspended in 1865.

It was this unfinished structure (with walls now rising 66 feet above the foundation) at Gervais and Main Streets that Sherman's raiders encountered on

South Carolina State House, Columbia
Lee Davis Perry

George Washington Monument at the South Carolina Statehouse (note the broken cane)
Lee Davis Perry

February 17, 1865, in their infamous assault on Columbia. This quintessential symbol of Secessionist South Carolina escaped the fires that consumed the old state house and most of the city, but it was an irresistible target for Yankee artillery. It was not until 1903 that the building itself was completed, and the business of the state finally found a home within its granite walls. The copper-domed building is beautifully restored today, but anyone visiting the site can still see the pockmarks from Union cannon fire defacing the west and southwest exterior walls. Each of the six marks is proudly commemorated with a bronze star.

Another less obvious scar visible on the steps of the State House concerns the elegant statue of President George Washington that faces Gervais Street and looks down Main where the fire once left a vast wasteland. Supposedly this life-size statue was the only one for which Washington himself posed during his lifetime. Only six bronze castings were made of the original marble sculpture, and this one was sent to South Carolina.

Unfortunately, the statue got its share of attention on that fateful night in 1865. The inscription tells us the Union forces "brickbatted it," breaking off the president's slender cane. He appears to lean confidently on a walking stick that ends mysteriously somewhere near his shin. The piece of the cane was thought to have disappeared in the rubble and confusion of the fire. Amazingly the broken piece turned up, but the statue of George Washington was never repaired. Today that piece is on display at the South Carolina Confederate Relic Room and Military Museum just a few blocks away from the State House grounds. His broken cane, like the artillery damage on the walls, was left for future generations to witness and contemplate the grim days at the end of the Civil War. Contemporary updates to the State House grounds include the removal in 2015 of the Confederate flag prominently displayed for 54 years, and an African American history monument added in 2001, the first such monument placed on any state's capitol grounds.

Chapter 5
THE UPSTATE

Burt-Stark Mansion
400 N. Main St., Abbeville; (864) 366-0166; burtstark.com; open for guided tours Fri and Sat afternoons; admission charged

There are a few names of towns or places that are indelibly and forever associated with great events in America's War Between the States: Harper's Ferry, Appomattox, Gettysburg, and, of course, Fort Sumter. The town of Abbeville does not ring a bell for most Americans, and, yet, Abbeville has been called "the birthplace and deathbed of the Confederacy." Ironically, Abbeville is one of the few towns in the state that escaped actual battle and survived the war largely unscathed.

The place most associated with the creation of the Confederacy is Charleston, where the Ordinance of Secession was signed and read to cheering throngs on the street. However, one month earlier on November 22, 1860, Abbeville hosted the initial meeting where seceding from the Union was the principal topic of discussion, and the plans for secession were first made. The meeting site was on a hill now called Secession Hill, which today is marked with a commemorative plaque, substantiating Abbeville's claim to be the birthplace of the Confederacy.

A similar misunderstanding exists concerning the technical end of the Confederate government. By the spring of 1865, the Confederacy was in a state of chaos and shambles. On April 18, Mrs. Jefferson (Varina) Davis, wife of the President of the Confederacy, fled Richmond, Virginia, and stopped in Abbeville to stay as a guest of old family friends, former US Congressman Armistead Burt and his wife, Martha Calhoun Burt. She was followed by a wagon train supposedly laden with the remaining gold from the Confederate treasury.

On May 2, a few days after Mrs. Davis's departure, President Davis himself arrived in Abbeville accompanied by his cabinet members and guarded by the remnants of five cavalry brigades that constituted what was left of the Confederate government at the time. They stopped at the Burt's home for one night and held what is said to be the last meeting of the war cabinet, where they made the decision to end armed resistance and cease hostilities against the North. This event in the front parlor of what is now called the Burt-Stark Mansion is the place in Abbeville where the Confederate government officially died. This fact may be largely overlooked today, but the role the mansion played in Civil War history led to its designation as a National Historic Landmark in 1992. Mary Stark Davis, last descendant of the

Burt-Stark Mansion, Abbeville
Lee Davis Perry

family, recognized the importance of her historic Greek Revival home and donated it and its furnishings to the Abbeville County Historic Preservation Commission for ongoing preservation. Visit the website or call ahead to confirm days and times for tours of the mansion.

Fort Hill (John C. Calhoun House)

102 Fort Hill St., Clemson; 864-656-2475; clemson.edu/forthill; open daily except major holidays and school closings; admission donation suggested

Fort Hill, prior to the Civil War, was the home of a famous public servant and states-man of note John Caldwell Calhoun. During his 40-year national political career he served as a US congressman, secretary of war and of state, vice president of the United States in two administrations, and a US senator from South Carolina. When not in Washington he resided with his wife, Floride, on the eleven-hundred-acre antebellum plantation from 1825 until his death in 1850. Calhoun wrote some of his most significant political papers onsite. Among them were his *South Carolina Exposition* and *Protest* (1828) expressing a philosophical rationale for nullification or the right of an individual state to declare federal legislation unconstitutional, and

Fort Hill (John C. Calhoun House), Clemson
Lee Davis Perry

the Fort Hill Address (1831) further delineating and defending nullification and states' rights.

The original 4-room house was built in 1803 by Hopewell-Keowee Church (now Old Stone Presbyterian Church) for their pastor, Dr. James McElhenny. It was called Clergy Hall and served as their manse or parsonage. Under Calhoun's tenure more acreage was acquired, and the house was expanded to fourteen rooms. An enslaved African American labor force was used to cultivate crops on the 450 acres of farmland and maintain the household and structures on the plantation. The property was renamed Fort Hill in honor of a Revolutionary-period fortification previously existing there. Architecturally, the house is Greek Revival style with Federal detailing. Of special interest among the furnishings is a mahogany sideboard made from wood from the USS *Constitution* given to Calhoun by his good friend Senator Henry Clay of Kentucky.

After Calhoun's death the property was divided among many family members until Calhoun's son-in-law, Thomas Green Clemson, inherited the majority of it in 1875. In his 1888 will, he gave more than 814 acres and $80,000 to the State of South Carolina for establishment of a public scientific and agricultural college there. He also stipulated that the house "shall never be torn down or altered; but shall be kept in repair with all articles of furniture and vesture . . . and shall always be open for inspection of visitors."

Today, Fort Hill, known also as the John C. Calhoun Mansion and Library, is made up of the main dwelling house, Calhoun's office and library, a reconstructed kitchen, and a springhouse. It sits in the middle of the Clemson campus and is surrounded by the many buildings of the school. Since the founding of Clemson Agricultural College (now Clemson University) in the 1890s, the school has upheld Thomas G. Clemson's requests by maintaining and operating Fort Hill as a house museum open to the public.

Ninety-Six and Star Fort
1103 Hwy. 248, Ninety-Six; 864-543-4068; nps.gov/ninetysix; open daily; free

Visitors to South Carolina are often puzzled when they see the town named "Ninety-Six" on their maps of Greenwood County in upstate South Carolina. This unusual name for a municipality always prompts the question, "How did it gets its name?" The romantic version is a favorite of many. It involves an Indian maiden who during the Cherokee War of the 1760s learned of an impending Indian attack on the British garrison. She supposedly rode ahead to the British camp to warn her English lover of the imminent danger. To mark her way, she named the streams along her route and found her soldier at the trading post at the ninety-sixth stream.

Ninety-Six and Star Fort
Lee Davis Perry

Romantic as this story may be, it seems far more plausible that another legend might be closer to the truth. This one tells of a surveyor general named George Hunter, who first mapped this area of the state in 1730. As he made his map, he marked the location "Ninety Six." It was assumed that meant it was 96 miles from the lower Cherokee Indian town of Keowee (near today's Clemson, South Carolina), and the name stuck. The trouble with that theory is, by contemporary measures, it simply isn't true. Ninety-Six isn't 96 miles from anywhere in particular. Whatever the truth is, this quirky name for the quiet southern town has endured and is likely to remain unchanged.

Historically, Ninety-Six played a role in the establishment of our nation. European settlement began in the early 1700s, but the Cherokee remained a threat and Fort Ninety-Six was constructed for the colonists' protection. Located at the crossroads of numerous backcountry trading routes, the village grew to include a dozen houses, taverns, shops, a courthouse, and jail. By 1775 the location was considered strategically important by both sides during the American Revolution. The 1st Battle of Ninety-Six took place that year, and it was the first land battle fought south of New England. After three days of fighting, a truce was called with no side admitting defeat. The site also contains the grave of James Birmingham, of present-day Abbeville County, who fell during this engagement. According to records kept at the time, Birmingham was the first southerner to die for his country in the American Revolution.

The British fortified the town in 1780 recognizing the need to control the area during their focus on the Southern Campaign. They used loyalist soldiers and enslaved people from area plantations and farms to construct an earthen, eight-point star-shaped fort with 14-foot-high walls. One thousand patriots led by Major General Nathanael Greene tactically set up a siege of Star Fort containing 550 loyalists defending Ninety-Six. The siege lasted from May 22 to June 19, 1781, making it the longest field siege of the Revolutionary War. During this time, the patriot forces dug siege lines while under fire from the fort. As word of a British relief column on its way reached Greene, he quickly ordered an unsuccessful assault on the stronghold. The patriots withdrew before the British arrived, but the British decided days later to abandon the location as well. Today, the well-preserved Star Fort is thought to be a prime example of an original 18th-century fortification and offers a unique, immersive experience in the warfare of the time.

Thematic Index

African American and Civil Rights History

Architectural Significance

Artists' and Writers' Sites

Civil War and Reconstruction Sites